How to Make Your Thoughts Disappear!

Your Guide to Crushing Obstacles on Your Path to Success

By Gary Coxe

How to Make Your Thoughts Disappear—Your Guide to Crushing Obstacles on Your Path to Success

Copyright © 2015 by Gary Coxe

ISBN-10: 0-692-41037-6
ISBN-13: 978-0-692-41037-0

Published by: Coxe's Enterprises.
GaryCoxe.com

Table of Contents

Chapter 1
HOW TO MAKE YOUR
THOUGHTS DISAPPEAR

This book isn't about simply controlling your thoughts. It's about taking your thoughts to another level where you can actually making them disappear. That's right…disappear!

Think about that—actually making your thoughts disappear. And how would that even be possible? More importantly, what would be the amazing benefits of having the ability to do something like that?

It's a known fact that thoughts create emotions; and emotions create actions; your actions in turn create results. Often, when we hear the word "results," we think of a positive outcome. But are all "results" good?

If we could make our thoughts disappear and if we could remove or control our negative emotions, at the very least, we should be able to interrupt them and stop them from taking us down negative or even destructive paths. What would something like that be worth to you? To me…it would be priceless.

This trail that leads from one thought to another can make a huge impact on either positive or negative thoughts throughout our lives. Our thoughts are that powerful. So then, our thoughts lead to our emotions. Have you ever had an emotion you didn't like? Who hasn't, right? Imagine removing your emotions by removing the thoughts that caused them. Are you beginning to see the power of this potential?

When working with the many clients I have had over the many years I have been doing this, I have heard people say they are their own worst enemies because their minds are often bombarded with

5

uncontrollable thoughts—thoughts they can neither harness nor control.

From as early as I can remember, I've been fascinated with the mind and how it can control us and how we should be able to control it. To this day, my fascination continues. A number of years ago, I experienced some incredible challenges in my life.

By far, those challenges were worse than the unbelievable tragedy that awaited me in the early part of adulthood, when my wife told me my baby wasn't mine, when my uncle was killed in a plane crash, my grandfather and stepfather both died of cancer, and my father was murdered. I had, unfortunately, experienced this and much more by the young age of 21. I'll get to more of that in a moment.

CHECK THIS OUT!

I invite you to view some websites offering amazing opportunities. Check them out when you have a minute...

To receive my FREE Daily Success Videos go to garycoxe.com

If you want to cure your fears or phobias visit cureyourfears.com

If you want to join me for 4 days for a private coaching in an intimate setting, learn more by going to beyondfirstclass.com

The last link I want you to look at is for my 4-step process in changing negative behavior and how to clean out your emotional hard drive: unbreakableselfesteem.com

I was raised in a fanatical religious sect so my beliefs in God were instilled in me from childhood. I made a very bold decision several decades later to totally leave this sect. The emotional and mental consequences of leaving that group were much greater than I had imagined they could have been. And this is why:

Once people leave this religion, all of their family and friends 'disown' them. They shun the deserters and will never talk to them again. Subsequently, I chose to get a divorce from an 18-year marriage, because I needed to cut all ties with this sect.

I had not planned for such a challenge. The best way I can describe it is that it's as if you were removed from ALL of the family and friends that you have known all your life, and then placed in a different country without being able to talk to or even see them again. I was not prepared for such an emotional roller coaster ride, nor have I ever experienced such pain before or since. And remember, I had experienced a lot of pain in my early life.

This new challenge was an obstacle I often wondered how I was going to overcome and live a successful life. I had never experienced anything like this and I knew it was going to take years to overcome. I started to spiral emotionally, had to borrow money to infuse into my business due to the challenge of coping. I was eventually nearly $400,000 in debt, and I had lost my whole support network that I'd had all my life...gone with one decision!

Today, I am beyond blessed to have made that decision and have turned my whole life around. The debt is gone and I am emotionally and mentally in a place that I never knew was humanly possible, this includes mastering the art of making my thoughts disappear.

Shortly after all of this happened, it was so challenging I found myself drinking a couple glasses of wine along with 3 to 5

7

Benadryl every night just to fall asleep. My thoughts and emotions where so uncontrollable I couldn't get a solid handle on them.

Then I started reading and came to a sentence in a book I don't even remember the name of, that briefly discussed meditation. The book said some meditation practitioners can make their thoughts disappear, but the book never discussed how it was done.

The possibility intrigued me to no end. Wow! I had never heard of such a thing. Make your thoughts disappear? Again, for just a moment, think about this concept of making your thoughts disappear. Imagine the power!

Meditation practitioners can make their thoughts disappear.

Think about what negative emotions do to us or how they affect us. Where do these negative emotions come from? Yes, from our thoughts.

For starters, increased blood pressure has been related to a lack of sleep. How many sleepless nights have you had because you couldn't turn off your mind? Then, there is a lack of sleep due to anxiety. I could go on and on with this.

Here is another one for you—insomnia. It affects up to 50% of the population. One of the things that causes people to lose sleep is that they can't shut off their mind…their thoughts don't disappear, but continue to race.

No one needs to tell you what that's like. There are thoughts of excitement, then there are thoughts of worry, anxiety…have you lost any sleep over any of those things? Who hasn't, right?

That often leads to taking medication, or drinking alcohol to get to sleep, neither of which really help for any length of time. Other people wait until they get tired enough to fall asleep. If you don't get tired until it's really late at night, then you wake up the next morning without having gotten enough sleep.

I soon began to realize that the reason I was drinking two glasses of wine every night was not because I was addicted to alcohol, but because I had so much mental and emotional stress. I needed something to slow down my thoughts that created all of the trouble.

I thought if I could learn to master 'making my thoughts disappear,' I would have more control, so I could literally shut down my mind and fall asleep. I believed I was onto something very powerful, so I set out to learn how to do it right.

I did a search on the internet, 'how to make your thoughts disappear,' and nothing came up.
Nothing at all. Now keep in mind, being from that religious sect, the word 'meditation' was a no-no, let alone entertaining the concept of making my thoughts disappear. However, since I was free from those chains, and was obsessed with learning how to do this, I set to figuring it out.

If I could 'make my thoughts disappear,' I could shut down my mind and fall asleep.

I knew enough about our minds and thoughts that I believed I could figure it out on my own—and I finally did it. Now, it's changed my entire life. About 30 days after I heard of such a concept, I was beginning to master it. From that point on, I stopped cold turkey with my previous routine of drinking two glasses of wine and taking pills to help me fall asleep. Then I began to realize not just the power of this technique, but also the unbelievable benefits.

What if you could choose what time you wanted to fall asleep? What if you could make your thoughts naturally disappear, or shut off the switch to your brain? You'd sleep like a snoring baby. I know this from my own personal experience because this is now what I do. It works because you're not thinking about anything else, so if you learn how not to 'think' about anything, you have nothing to worry about that will keep you up at night. You can even slow down your racing mind so much that it totally checks out for the night and you fall into blissful sleep.

How often have you found yourself deep in worry, or for that matter, extremely excited about something, and because of that excitement, your mind was racing with thoughts that still prevented you from going to sleep?

Though the excitement is keeping you from falling asleep, you still may need the sleep. So now you must be able to make those thoughts disappear and control the time you decide to fall asleep.

Though I'm not a doctor, common sense through my own life experiences tells me the reason people are so stressed out, is they are losing control. They can't get a good night's sleep because they are unable to control how they think—and when to stop thinking.

Here is a clearer picture…

You've started your day early, and as life begins to unfold, it's not all perfect. There are days that our levels of stress take us beyond our boiling point. The kids have to be ready for school, traffic jams force us to slow down, you spill coffee on your new clothes, bills are piling up and you don't have enough income to pay them, you encounter rude and insensitive people everywhere you go, your personal relationships become extra challenging and after about 12 hours of all this, your mind is consumed with worry, stress, and racing thoughts of how to deal with all of it.

You look for some kind of relief, knowing you're going to fall asleep late and when you finally do, at best, you toss and turn for the rest of the night. To get the relief you need, some people get a drink or a pill or some other way of finding artificial and temporary relief.

I recently came across an article from WebMD about the cost of losing sleep. I hope this will convince you that what I'm saying can change your life forever, as it did mine.

A 2007 study conducted in Great Britain found that people who got between five and seven hours of sleep each night nearly doubled their risk of death from all causes related to stress. The rate of deaths from cardiovascular disease doubled when people got only five hours of sleep each night.

Sleep-deprived people are more apt to demonstrate poor judgment and have the largest problem evaluating themselves and their abilities appropriately when they are sleep deprived. People who get six hours of sleep actually believe they have adapted to less sleep. However, test scores show they are less effective and less efficient during days following nights of just six hours of sleep.

One form of torture that has been used down through the centuries is sleep deprivation. The longer a person is forced to go without sleep, the less they can determine the difference between reality and fiction. Sleep deprivation is an extreme technique in interrogation of getting a subject to tell their secrets because they stop caring about the consequences, they fear they are going crazy and they will trade almost anything for just a few hours' sleep.

Traffic accidents involving sleep-deprived drivers are higher when they only get five to six hours of sleep. They are more likely to simply rest their eyes and end up falling asleep at the wheel, whether just at a red light, caught in a traffic jam or even while driving down the highway.

The current fad of using energy drinks to remain awake longer and sleep less at night is showing an increase in the number of accidents in the work place, in the home or behind the wheel of a motor vehicle. Although users of energy drinks are able to remain awake longer in the day, they are less able to focus their attention on one task at a time—such as driving—and are more prone to have or cause accidents. This probably would not be so bad if the users were the only ones hurt, but all too often, accidents injure or even kill innocent people who, themselves, are getting enough sleep, but who are unable to get out of the way of a frantic person who's focusing on three or four things simultaneously—only one of which is driving.

Loss of sleep seems to be associated with greater hunger and larger appetite and is even related to obesity. A study conducted in 2004 found that people who sleep less than six hours each night were almost 30 percent more likely to gain weight as compared with people who slept seven to nine hours every night. That makes perfect. If people are only sleeping for five hours, then they are awake for 19 hours each day and that gives them more time to munch, to snack and eat their way to obesity.

Possibly the biggest example of the financial losses due to lack of sleep is demonstrated by individuals elected to office and given the responsibility of spending the peoples' tax money judiciously. When they are sleep deprived, they are less likely to make good decisions and are more likely to make bad decisions, or in the worst case, fall asleep during a vote which ends up spending tax money on frivolous or totally unnecessary bills—and they never know what hit them until it is too late.

Loss of sleep seems to be associated with greater hunger, larger appetite and obesity.

These are just some of the things that insomnia costs you. Now think of the benefits of being able to make your thoughts disappear, so you can control this—at least the part of it that directly affects you.

In this book, I will focus a lot on the benefits of a good night's rest. By understanding more about how we think, we can control our thoughts to the point of making them disappear. If you are not mentally weighed down by the thoughts in your mind, they won't keep you awake and you will be able to get a good night's sleep.

I will also share with you how to use these techniques any time during your day. I will show you ways to be more consciously aware of your own thoughts and emotions so you can learn to control them instead of allowing them to control you.

I will focus on the benefits of controlling your thoughts to help you fall asleep so you can see the importance of learning to do it yourself. You will get amazing results, just like I did. Keep in mind, all of my adult life I have never been able to sleep well. I already know the side effects of a lack of sleep and, most probably, so do you. By mastering how to make my thoughts disappear, I have experienced benefits beyond my wildest dreams...no pun intended :).

Not only will you receive the benefits of more sleep and being able to control when you sleep and for how long you want to sleep, you will also learn to understand how these processes can help you control your emotions. After all, emotion is the basis of all the good and all the bad in the world.

There are so many benefits to learning to control your emotions that every one of us has experienced at least some of them in our lives. If we could all control our emotions better, we would find ourselves living in a completely different world.

-There would be no such thing as Road Rage.
-There would be no child or spousal abuse.
-There would less of a need for homeless and battered spouse shelters.
-There would be no crimes of passion.
-The numbers of suicide would almost disappear.
-The numbers of psychological diseases would diminish due to less emotional stress.
-The prison populace would be greatly diminished in numbers.
-Teachers would have fewer discipline problems in the classroom.
-There would be no such saying as 'Going Postal.'
-There would be less anger among teenagers and fewer gangs, gang wars, examples of graffiti and vandalism.

-The word 'revenge' would become something of the past.

-There would be fewer alcoholics and fewer drug addicts.
-Society would be able to concentrate its resources on creating better things in life rather than spending them on feeding and housing the homeless, destitute and prisoners.
-There would not be any need for those TV commercials that show abused puppies and kittens.
-Overall, there would be greater understanding and fewer examples of the bad things in life.

As a person who is extremely fast paced and constantly on the go at 100 mph an hour (that's a metaphor, not the speed of my driving), I know the dangers of not being able to sleep peacefully. It's pretty cool getting to bed and slamming on the brakes from that fast pace and going from Drive to Park in a matter of minutes. Then to wake up mentally clear, with no after-effects from pills or alcohol to get out of bed and turn on life's after-burner all over again after a restful night of natural and uninterrupted sleep—every night.

Emotion is the basis of all the good and all the bad in the world.

I will forewarn you. If you are looking for a quick fix, this is NOT it! What I will share with you in this book will seem very simple at times, but it is not easy. If you are into being the best you can be, improving your relationships and lifestyle, then this will be for you. This is a lifestyle. It takes lots of patience and effort and gives fantastic results.

Look at it this way. Up until now, have you ever heard of the concept of making your thoughts disappear? Probably not. Consider this, as well. For your entire life, each and every night over and over and over, you probably have never stopped and said, 'Okay, I am now going to make my thoughts disappear.' So this is not part of your normal thought processes or your everyday behavior. After beginning, you might choose to give up...but don't. This is powerful stuff. It takes commitment and practice—and lots of it.

I think of the statement in the original movie "Karate Kid," 'wax on, wax off.' The young boy learned the waxing techniques which were indirectly teaching his muscles the karate blocking and striking techniques. When the karate sparring actually began, he found it easier to learn.

There will be certain disciplines you must learn to master before you can come close to learning to 'make your thoughts disappear.' As we continue in this book, I will introduce you to certain key 'wax on and wax off' principles I have found that, once I understood and mastered them, made this process of making my thoughts disappear, much easier.

This is not a quick fix process until you learn to master it, and you won't be able to do it right away. In fact, most people will give up before they master the process. Keep in mind the direct benefits making your thoughts disappear will do for you and let those benefits be your motivating factors. Learn this. Master this, and make a better life for yourself.

Though I will be focusing on how to use these techniques to put the brakes on your thinking and to assist you in getting better sleep, we'll be discussing how to use them throughout your day, as well.

For me, I'm at the point where it is natural for me to get into bed, make a conscious decision when I want to fall asleep and to do so—immediately. That's control. I love to be in control of my life and my thoughts. This will take it to a new level for you. So be patient and make a commitment to master this and it will change your life!

I truly believe that most people, though they say they are aware of the power of their minds and their thoughts, they really do not understand the true power of what they possess as human beings. I invite you to be curious, be open-minded and approach this with the understanding that the benefits of mastering these processes, beyond the part of just making your thoughts disappear, will help you fall asleep all night, every night. The possibilities and the benefits are truly endless.

Chapter 2
AWAKEN YOUR AWARENESS

For starters, I don't know how familiar you may be with my background. I barely finished high school and that's the extent of my education. You'll obviously note I may be talking a lot about meditation and our thought processes throughout this book. I also have no formal training in psychology or meditation practices. This book is a very raw layman's description of meditation or, at the very least, I've put it together in a way that works for me and can also work for you. I may not be the most creative person in the world, but I do love discovering what's out there. I also enjoy trying to make already established and accepted systems more effective and efficient, when I can. That doesn't mean I have improved on traditional forms of meditation. But I have found some additional techniques that work well with what we have in the 21st century. What I do know is, this system works for me and I have found it to be extremely powerful.

The first basic step in learning how to make your thoughts disappear is to become totally aware of what is going on within you—your mind and body—consciously being in the present at all times. If you are not totally aware of yourself, you cannot begin to respond to the need to make quick changes—or much change at all, for that matter.

When a person is not totally aware of the things that trigger certain actions, reactions, thoughts and feelings, life will ultimately control them instead of them controlling their life. Being aware of what triggers certain thoughts and feelings is the start of controlling and changing them, whenever necessary.

The first step in learning how to make your thoughts disappear is becoming totally aware of what is going on within you.

We live in an instant-gratification society. We want everything to be fixed overnight. And why not? We see cities destroyed and rebuilt in a one-hour television show. We see armies raised and weapons built to save the world in a two-hour movie. Why shouldn't we expect these things to be real in our mundane lives? We want quick fixes for everything and this expectation can be one of the biggest obstacles to our personal success.

Here is a typical example that will probably shock you. Take a guess at what the fast growing demographics of mood-enhancing medications are in the world today? Preschoolers! Can you imagine that? Preschoolers are the fastest-growing users of mood-enhancing medications in our society. For me, the thought that comes to mind is, how are adults allowing themselves to justify this? And what about the doctors who prescribe them to these small children?

I believe it's because of a lack of accountability and not wanting to take ownership of a problem—any problem. It's called the Quick Fix Syndrome, or QFS. We often go into this excuse mode to justify such easy but unnecessary solutions. I'm sure you've heard this before.

I want to discuss depression among children, then children are depressed because they come from broken homes and are sometimes left to themselves for several hours until the single parent returns home from work. Children see all the good things in the world on television, and then have to look at their miserable lives when TV is turned off. They may see a stream of strangers entering and leaving their home and have trouble with the uncertainty of having to adapt to that situation. They listen to the older kids in the neighborhood talk about committing crimes and taking what they want, but the little ones don't have the means of getting any of those items which they think they want.

"My child just won't listen to me. He is so hyperactive, he's bouncing of the walls. His teacher can't even control him in school. He can't focus on one single thing at a time. I'm not a doctor. I don't know how to slow him down. That's why doctors make the big bucks. Let them take care of my child. It's obviously a medical problem. I already have enough problems of my own." The list of excuses some parents make may even include some valid excuses on why they allow doctors to prescribe depressants for their 3-year-olds. But is that really the best way to handle the problem? Is it the only way? Absolutely not to both questions! There are both more ways and better ways to help children with hyperactivity problems or lack of concentration problems that we need to consider.

The quick fix is meds and it's even easier to justify once the child or adult starts taking them, because they actually 'work.' Give any child or adult a pill or an alcoholic drink and of course it's going to slow them down. But just because it slows them down and they seem to focus better, that doesn't solve the core issue.

The Quick Fix Syndrome—QFS—is the simple bandage on the large wound that doesn't come close to solving the problem.

It doesn't stop there. What about the doctors who give out the prescriptions as if they were candy? Again, it's the QFS, the simple bandage on the large wound that doesn't come close to solving the problem. My point in sharing this with you is that, if a person is always learning to look for and settle for these easy and cheap solutions, it becomes an internal conflict when they decide they want total self- mastery—including the powerful self-mastery of making your thoughts disappear. I consider myself incredibly aware of my thoughts, actions and emotions. But even still, I occasionally catch myself unconsciously going down a path that isn't taking me in the direction I need and want to go.

This is part of the 'wax on wax off' mindset. You have to set the right mindset in place and that's what I am doing with you right now. Mastering the techniques in this book will only come from having the right mindset and making what I am sharing with you a way of life—not just a quick fix, but an honest to goodness life-altering technique.

I believe I speak from experience. After going through all the many tragedies in my life, I was taking the meds; I was drinking the alcohol. It was extremely difficult for me to cope with my problems. I was an emotional wreck. I believe, if I had run to a doctor or a shrink with my issues every time I wanted to cry, I would have been diagnosed with just about every psychiatric problem under the sun—including Post Traumatic Stress Disorder (PTSD), incidental depression, inability to cope, with suicidal tendencies, and the list would go on and on.

Total awareness of self, along with changing your belief system can make monumental changes in your life. I often wear a wrist band we offer on our website that reads, 'Wherever I am, at I'm not at my potential.' My awareness—and frequent reminder—of this thought does a lot for me. Though I know I would probably be diagnosed as having Attention Deficit Hyperactive Disorder (ADHD), I refuse to pigeon hole myself in that box. Here is a typical example. People may tell you there is such a thing as writer's block. That's a limited thought. As I'm writing this for you right now, I had planned on setting this time aside days ago to do this. If I don't feel like writing, oh well, I have to write anyway. I need to write for at least four hours straight, today.

Total awareness of self, along with changing our belief system can make monumental changes in our lives.

If I feel like only writing for two hours, it's not enough. I need to write for four hours. If I decide to throw in the towel after two hours I can, but I choose not to do so. If I bought into the ADHD thing, then that would allow me to validate the diagnosis of ADHD and I would be able to quit after two hours—with a clear conscience.
So I have decided to change my story and simply tell myself, 'Wherever I'm at (wanting to stop writing at two hours), I'm not at my potential (write for two additional hours, or more). With this kind of awareness, and a solid belief to go with it, I'm able to break through as many mental limitations or mental stereotypes that get in my way. So, I'll keep my 'ADHD' for flying airplanes, where I'm always multi-tasking and moving around, pushing buttons, flipping switches and doing ten things at a time.

I'm always very careful what I buy into and what I choose to believe or not believe. It can be very easy to believe what you've been told to believe, or what you have told yourself to believe. Because of this lack of awareness, we often throw common sense out of the window along with our ability to reason.

WE DECIDE WHAT TO LIKE AND DISLIKE AT AN EARLY AGE

Here is a powerful reason why or how this happens. If you meet some who is richer than you are, or like myself have written books or been on TV, in your mind, you will place a higher status on that person, higher than perhaps they deserve. And if you're not careful, you'll believe everything they say. Then, if you're not careful, you will become a sheep being led to the slaughter. To prove that, at one time, just about everyone on the planet used to believe the earth was flat. Cult leader Jim Jones took nearly 1,000 people to their death because they bought into the beliefs he convinced them to believe and they all committed suicide with his potassium cyanide-laced Koolaid®. So, don't think you're immune to buying or believing things that simply aren't true or that don't make sense.

I recall the new excitement I had when I left the sect I had been in. I was finally able to think for myself and openly express myself, question my beliefs and not profess to believe something just because I had been told to believe it all my adult life. When I started questioning so many other things in life, I came to discover so much more about myself. I assure you there are some things about yourself that you haven't uncovered yet and I hope this book will enable you to do that.

Here is a great example of that. For a few years after leaving the sect, I had been chatting over the phone with a young lady. Because of her height, she was always tuned in to people's height and very aware of it. She was 5'10". When we finally met face to face, she asked me how tall I was. I told her I was 6'1". She replied, "No way. You can't be." I insisted that I was.

She challenged me to get a measuring tape, which I did. We measured and I am actually 6'2". I was quite surprised. I wondered how in the world that had happened. Then, after some thought, I figured it out. My height is on my driver's license and my pilot's license. I looked at my pilot's license and it read 6'1". I looked at my driver's license and it read 6'2". Every one to two years I have to renew my pilot's license under my instructor certificate. I've always said my height was 6'1" because I 'know' that from renewing my pilot's license as often as I do.

However, my driver's license is only renewed once every ten years and that's why I never pay attention to the height and I only look at it once every 10 years. Isn't that interesting? The moral of the story is, don't believe everything you believe.

Here is another interesting observation about how we believe things that are not necessarily true. All my life I have hated broccoli. It makes me gag. Just the smell of it turns my stomach. Think of a food that, as a child, you hated. Well, if you've hated that food from childhood, the chances are that, as an adult, you haven't tried that food again, since you were a child.

Don't believe everything you believe.

So, how do you really know you still hate that food? Mostly because you've told yourself you hate it over and over for decades. You've programmed yourself to believe you hate it. What's interesting about the power of our beliefs is that, when we begin to believe something, our brain seems to constantly look for ways to validate those beliefs whether they're true or not. This creates a reinforcement of your beliefs and makes them that much more real to you.

Then, one day, I decided to find out if I still really hate broccoli, or if I have just been programming myself for all these years. Of course, if you hated a food as a child, when you think of trying that food again, the first thing you will do is contort your face, 'Oh, that's gross!' So, I got the broccoli ready and made sure I wasn't going to screw up my face, like I'd done all my life just thinking about it. I took a bite and it was nothing like I had programmed myself to believe. It really wasn't that bad. Now, I won't tell you broccoli is my favorite food, but I don't have a problem eating it any more.

I wonder what foods you have programmed yourself to avoid for many years, that maybe if you give it a try, you might have a new and enjoyable experience? Seriously, think about it and give it a try. I'll discuss in a later chapter how you've actually used your nervous system in such a way that you've trained it to cause you not to like certain foods.

Then, what comes to mind next? If we've actually programmed ourselves to believe something simple like not eating certain foods, then we might wonder about all the other things we believed that have not been true all our lives.

I hope I'm making my point clear. Be careful what you believe to be true. I also encourage you to keep an open mind when reading this book. Without total awareness of what is going on around you, regardless of what you do or don't believe, it's hard to be free from prejudices against other things or other people.

FEEL THE SAND

I have a good friend whose name is Dean. Dean can free dive to depths of 75 feet or more and stay underwater for up to five minutes straight. That is not an easy task. But he didn't learn this skill overnight. He was actually taught how to do this by a world famous diver. Anyone can be taught the skills to do that, though the outcome may be different and vary from person-to-person.

Here is how Dean was taught. First of all, here is not how he was taught. He didn't learn to do this by going into the water and holding his breath for longer periods each time he dove, making an attempt to increase his time under water. That would only seem to make sense.

His mentor actually brought him to the beach and dug a hole for him that was big enough for him to fit into it. Then, he placed the sand all over his body so he was exposed only from his neck up. Then, his teacher poured water over the sand that was covering his chest. This caused the sand to become very heavy on his chest. One might wonder, what was the purpose of doing this? The answer is quite interesting.

The water over the sand made the sand much heavier. Every time Dean breathed in and out, the weight of the sand caused his inhaling and exhaling to become more difficult.

He felt the smallest amount of movement, when breathing in and out, because of the weight of the wet sand on his chest. You could say he became hyper-aware or hyper-sensitive to these movements. Even though he knew before hand, this exercise was all about learning to control his breathing.

This, then, created a tremendous awareness of how to be more sensitive to his breathing process while under controlled stress. The controlled stress, in this case, was the extra weight of the sand and the water against his chest.

Awareness is so powerful. To me it's a way of life and using it is like a muscle. The concept of awareness can be like an exercise and you can become proficient at it. Here is a very powerful example of this.

Awareness is a way of life and using it is like a muscle.

ECHO-LOCATION ON A BIKE

Years ago, I watched a TV segment of a young boy in his teens who was born totally blind. What made this interview really amazing is that this boy was riding a bicycle through the streets without any assistance. Keep in mind, he's totally blind. How in the world did he learn to do that? He used his ears. That's right, he used his ears—to see.

He would get on his bike and make clicking sounds from his mouth, then, much like a bat uses its own built in radar system, he trained himself to listen to where and how the sounds he made. Clicks remade with his tongue bounced off the things around him and then returned to him. This is how he guided himself through the streets, in between parked cars and other objects in the neighborhood. How amazing!

In fact, he actually started teaching other blind people how to do the same thing. To me, that's fascinating. There is so much human potential we have not yet learned to tap into. According to this young boy, anyone can learn how to do this echo-location. For most people, they will never learn such a skill because they are not blind nor are they forced to learn it. If you were to become blind, there could be a chance you might want to check him out and learn how he does it. I can assure I would. It could be that important to many of us.

27

It's my hope that you find this information as important as I have stated. It's hard for me to even explain to you the amazing sleep I have each night. Keep in mind, while on tour, I can end up sleeping in three or four different beds and as many hotels, in less than a week—not to mention the emotional control and the health benefits that come along with this getting a good night's sleep.

In the previous three years alone, while writing this book, I have given over 600 presentations. As I mentioned all the traveling to different cities, sleeping in different hotels and different beds, this has been one of the keys to maintaining this fast-paced lifestyle.

There is so much human potential we have not yet learned to tap into.

I will continue to discuss the benefits of getting more and better sleep by using my technique, but this is just the tip of the iceberg when we include the emotional and mental control you will also be learning to enjoy in this book.

As we continue through the rest of the book, we'll discuss my techniques with the goal to preparing the body by preparing the mind to start slowing down in order to begin making your thoughts disappear. Let's not stop here. The fun is just beginning.

Chapter 3
HOW TO LIVE TO BE 256 YEARS OLD

There was a Chinese herbalist by the name of Li Qing Yun who supposedly lived to be over 256 years old, though this is not totally confirmed. Some records seem to indicate that he lived to 197 years old.

Either way you look at it, it's a pretty long run. But I read something that he was supposedly to have said just before he died about his key to living such a long life was. He said to, "Keep a quiet heart, sit like a tortoise, walk sprightly like a pigeon, and sleep like a dog."

To understand more of this, it's important to get a grasp of the oriental culture and lifestyle. Keep in mind I'm setting you up right now for your 'Wax on, Wax off' process.

Let's break up some of what Yun might have meant by this statement. First, was to 'keep a quiet heart.' In this book, you may note that I refer to it as being 'still of heart.'

KEEPING A QUIET HEART HELPS PROMOTE EMOTIONAL HEALTH

What does it mean to "keep a quiet heart" from the perspective of acupuncture and Oriental medicine? The energy of the cardiovascular system is related to the element of Fire. Fires can burn out of control, just as emotions can. Unchecked emotions and stress directly affect the heart. Common signs relating to disharmony of the heart include palpitations, insomnia and general anxiety. I've already shared some of this as you'll recall from the previous chapters.

29

When the heart is in balance, joy is the natural state, and intimate relationships grow and strengthen with ease. A person with a balanced, quiet heart can live a longer life than one whose heart is in a state of disharmony.

"Keep a quiet heart, sit like a tortoise, walk sprightly like a pigeon, and sleep like a dog."

Here's a simple concept that will help you become motivated to learn and master the principles in this book. Keep in mind, you already often focus on what you value or claim to be important to you. If you haven't placed at least a very high value on your health, you'll walk away from this book and give up all too easily. Just because someone says their health is important to them, doesn't mean their actions reflect that value. Most adults in our society understand the concept of avoiding whatever might injure their health. But actually living a life in which we eat all of the best foods, engage in all the best activities and follow the instructions of our health professionals is very difficult because other priorities frequently get in our way.

Several things fuel me to be passionate about this material. I love controlling my mind as much as I possibly can. I like to play games with it instead of allowing it to play games with me. Second, I appreciate the possession of amazingly good health. I'm very blessed to be extremely healthy. I do, however, know it has been good as a result of my choices with regards to what and how I eat or how I respond to stressors in my life. I have learned to 'keep a quite heart.'

Each year or so, I have to get a flight physical to maintain my pilot's license. I recall two comments from the medical staff on two different occasions. Once, the nurse took my after vitals and asked, 'While I was checking your heart beat you slowed it down, didn't you?' I smiled. I'm often able to lower my heart to beat to the low 50's, or below. It comes from having a quiet heart. On another occasion, after the doctor took my blood pressure, he said I have the blood pressure of a teenager. This isn't by chance or even by genetics. I see the value as you do in having great health. It doesn't only come from eating the right foods and exercising regularly. It comes from learning how to 'keep a quite heart.'

In our next chapter, I'll share with you ways we have programmed ourselves not to keep a quiet heart. If you're not aware of how this happens and how you can improve your health, then that task will be more difficult for you, not to mention you won't be starting from a position of alignment, being able to make your thoughts disappear.

LESSONS FROM A TORTOISE THAT REDUCE STRESS AND IMPROVE AWARENESS.

Meditation is of primary importance to health and longevity. Sitting and meditating as a daily practice is, effectively, sitting like a tortoise.

A quiet, yet active practice, meditation requires mental stamina and strong will power and cultivates self-awareness. By sitting for daily meditation practice, you can better let go of your fears. You can accept the inevitable changes which occur internally as you age, and also accept changes in the outside world. The acceptance you gain through meditation includes the acceptance of your own mortality.

Meditation requires mental stamina and strong will power and cultivates self-awareness.

The kidneys are associated with willpower and especially with the emotion of fear. Through meditation, you can cultivate the will power required to sit still, and also develop the personal strength of will necessary to confront the ceaseless thoughts and emotions of the mind.

Recently I read an article about the habits of successful people. In the article, it mentioned that Oprah Winfrey is a big proponent of quiet time. I am also a firm believer of this. This lesson was taught to me in a specific season in life like no other.

As of the writing of this book I have been in hotels all over the world for three years—each and every day. I have never in my life been by myself so much. There is no question that in the last three years, I have been by myself more than in any other time of my life. The lessons I have learned in that experience have been priceless.

I have performed nearly 600 hundred full presentations in this very short time as I previously mentioned. The stress level associated with traveling so much, mostly alone, and living in hotels is out of sight. I refused to give up, so I had to master the ability to reduce my stress and increase my mental awareness, yet not slow down and all the while stay focused. I often forced myself, twice a day, to just sit down, close my eyes and do nothing. I'll discuss more about this as we continue.

When was the last time you made it a regular, daily habit to simply sit in total quiet and do nothing, absolutely nothing? Doing it especially because you choose to do it, not because you think you have to due to the stresses of life.

You will be shocked at the benefits of doing this regularly—just twice a day for five minutes each time. People run themselves so ragged and keep their lives so hectic they can't give themselves five minutes of 'quiet, me time.' If you value your good health, and you really want to slow things down in your life, this practice is a must. Not only does it help me manage stress but it also helps me keep a quiet heart.

I recall one day on my travels I was pulling into a small parking lot to get groceries. A lady was pulling out of her parking space while her husband was with her. Because the parking lot was so small, and as I was pulling in the same lane coming from the opposite direction, I gave her more than enough room to leave the parking spot, but I was on the left side of the narrow row, not the right side because of such a tight space.

Her husband didn't seem to like what I did and, as they drove by, he rolled down his window and threw hot coffee against my car. I was able to remain still of heart. Not a change in heartbeat, not a fowl word, no negative emotion. But I worried about his peace of mind at being so angry over such a small incident.

Stop and think about how often you or someone you know loses emotional control in just one day. Imagine the unnecessary stress this puts on the body—and the mind.

Have you stopped to take the time to personally define for yourself what emotional control really is? For me, when I'm experiencing negative feelings or emotions I'm not keeping a quiet heart. I say negative because I'm okay at not having a quiet heart for fun, exiting, positive things. That promotes endorphins and many other positive internal responses.

WALKING SPRITELY LIKE A PIGEON HELPS TO INCREASE VITALITY

What does it mean to "walk spritely like a pigeon"? The spirited strut of a pigeon gives the impression of vitality, confidence and overall awareness. The pigeon is very aware of its environment and is ready to move or fly at a moment's notice.

The spritely quality of the pigeon's mobility represents the energy of the liver organ system. The force a seed needs to sprout and break through the earth as it grows in the spring is a great analogy for the energy of the liver system as every spring brings about new growth and new life.

The spirited strut of a pigeon gives the impression of vitality, confidence and overall awareness.

From the perspective of acupuncture and Oriental medicine, you need a healthy liver system for greater vitality. It is believed that any situation that constrains or frustrates a person will consequently injure the person's liver. In order for an aging person to remain healthy and creative, the body and mind must continue to be active. You must engage in new activities so that creativity and curiosity can flow freely and easily as you move through life.

Many people aren't even aware that they are not aware of what is good for them. It's my goal to dramatically increase your awareness by the time you finish this book. I do believe you'll experience a level of awareness you've never considered before. You won't be able to make your thoughts disappear if you don't experience the benefits of doing it at least once.

RELEASE WORRIES AND RESTORE ENERGY BY SLEEPING LIKE A DOG

What does it mean to "sleep like a dog?" A dog falls asleep easily and sleeps very deeply, awakening fully restored. Regular, restorative sleep is a key to feeling young, healthy and vital. In

order to sleep deeply and easily, like a dog, the body and m
must willingly power down. When you master much of what
share with you, you'll be able to control when you want to powe
down.

It can be very challenging in today's busy world to let go of your
daily worries and concerns in order to sink into a deep, restorative
sleep.

If your sleep is peaceful and you awaken feeling refreshed, this
indicates your heart is balanced, your kidneys are strong and your
liver energy flows freely. The more nights you have during which
you sleep like a dog, the younger you will look and feel.

A healthy mind and body need not decline with age. Prevention of
age-related cognitive and physical issues involves safeguarding the
yin, yang, and jing (adrenals, hormone balance, and genetic
endowments) throughout your lifespan by maintaining a healthy
diet, an active lifestyle, avoiding toxins, keeping harmony in your
environment and in your relationships, and maintaining an even
balance of activity and rest.

A healthy mind and body need not decline with age.

As brought to your attention in a previous chapter, the benefits of a
good night's sleep are priceless. My goal is get you to sleep like a
dog or even better, like a pampered baby.

It's time now to begin more of the 'wax on, wax off' process, so
here we go.

Chapter 4
NERVOUS SYSTEM
& THE DIFFERENCE
IMAGINATION AND
REALITY.

In this chapter, I will share with you my secret weapon. The secret weapon I have been using for years to help control change and behavior. It's perhaps one of the most powerful concepts I have ever used to change other peoples' behavior and certainly my own behavior, as well.

It's an in-depth understanding of the human body's nervous system. It is said that the nervous system can't tell the difference between the imagination and reality. This is so very true about the peripheral nervous system. Of course, the central nervous system can tell the difference, because the main part of the central nervous system is your brain. Understanding this one concept and learning how to apply it in your daily life is a real game changer. It's certainly done so for me.

The central nervous system can't tell the difference between imagination and reality.

Let's take some more time to understand this. When we create a thought, we often create a picture in our minds to accompany that thought without even realizing we are doing it. Have you ever had a thought that was a negative assumption about a situation or person and you continued down that path, just carrying on about the subject? Well, if the subject was negative, I'm sure many things started to happen with your body.

Your heart rate may have increased, your palms might have started sweating, and your blood pressure might have increased, your anxiety level could have also increased. You may have even gotten angry. And all of this happened because you started with a negative thought or a negative story. As you started thinking about the story, your nervous system couldn't tell the difference between imagination and reality. So your mind took over and your emotions let themselves to becoming so vivid it felt real.

Then, what often happens when you find out your assumptions weren't true? In time, your heart starts to slow down and you become calmer again.

It's no different than if I told you to imagine my fingernails are long and I scratched them across a dry chalkboard. Though there really is no chalkboard, most people would react by cringing, or with some similar body movement because just thinking about the fingernails scratching against a dry chalkboard creates a response. The reason? The nervous system can't tell the difference between imagination and reality. I want you to become a master at controlling your nervous system.

Let me go a bit overboard with another example. Let's imagine we are talking with someone who does not know how to swim. We are with them at a very large swimming pool. We tell them we are going to throw them into the middle of the pool and their goal will be to save themselves from drowning. They will have no flotation device, and nothing else to grab onto.

Just the mere thought of something like this, to someone who does not swim, would emotionally cripple them, bringing them to shear panic. But I only placed a simple thought in their mind. The nervous system can't tell the difference between imagination and reality. Just the thought of being thrown into the swimming pool takes control of every cell in their body.

I could just be kidding, simply mentioning this idea to them without any intention of throwing them into the pool. If that person could learn to be both consciously and consistently aware of how to take control of their life instead of allowing their thoughts to negatively engage their nervous system, they would be able to make drastic and dramatic changes.

Stay with me on this. I could take that person, if they were willing, and just by showing them how to train their nervous system, so they could respond positively, they could be thrown into the pool and still save their own life.

I understand this book isn't a manual on learning how to swim, but I want you to see the depths of how powerful so much of this is and how it can be so beneficial in so many areas of life. I'm primarily sharing these principles with you so you can apply them in all areas of your life.

People don't often drown because they can't swim. They drown because they panic. Similarly, people don't die because they choke on food, they die because, when they got food lodged in their throat, they immediately panicked, which instantly caused them to suck in more air through their mouth, thus lodging the food farther down their throat, rather than being totally and instantly aware of their problem and simply breathing through their nose.

People don't often drown because they can't swim. They drown because they panic.

I could train the person who doesn't know how to swim to not panic, by training or programming their nervous system to respond appropriately. Then I could teach them, once they are thrown into the pool, to simply sink to the bottom, bend their knees, and when they touch bottom, forcefully explode upward, back toward the surface. Once above the surface, they would take in more air and return to the bottom of the pool to do it again, several more times if necessary, until they get to the swallow end of the pool.

Stop for a moment and think how many times you lose some kind of control because you're not mentally in a place of total awareness. Someone pushes in front of you in a line at the store, and you respond negatively. Someone else looks at you the wrong way and again you respond in a negative manner.

While someone else is driving down the road, they see a small spider inside their car and they lose total control and end up having an accident. Things like this happen every day. Much of this negative programming happens when we aren't really paying attention and we don't even notice it.

Here is a powerful example of this. Let's say you and I are watching TV one night and we have a 2 year old child watching with us. All three of us are watching a show about the forest. As we are watching the TV screen, in the forest we see a huge snake sliding along the ground. Shortly afterward, the two year old is put to bed.

Several hours later, we end up frantically running to the child's room because he is screaming at the top of his lungs after a nightmare. The child doesn't understand and isn't old enough to communicate what happened and why he's screaming, so we'll never know about the nightmare. If we were able to watch the dream or nightmare that caused the child to scream so loudly, we would probably notice the child was dreaming about the snake he had seen on TV before going to bed. But now, in his dreams, the snake has wrapped itself around the boy and started to swallow him. The imagination or dream was so real, at that very moment, the child woke up screaming.

I can assure you at this point and in most cases, this child will now be phobic about snakes for the rest of his life and may not know what happened or why, or even remember how he became phobic. So three months later or three years later the child sees another snake, either on TV or in real life, and now instantly, without even having to think about it, he gets a flashback to the nightmare and totally freaks out. As the parents, we have no idea why the child responded so negatively about the snake. We just now associate that, 'My child is afraid of snakes.'

What actually happened was that dream, associated with such strong emotion, though it wasn't real, instilled a negative feeling toward snakes.

The younger we are, the less we understand how to control our nervous systems or how to avoid negative reactions which aren't good options.

There is an emotional and mental danger here for the child. Every time he sees or even thinks of a snake, because the nervous system can't tell the difference between imagination and reality, the fear digs its grave deeper and deeper until it is ingrained as a phobia of snakes. His brain is now wired to validate and reemphasize this belief, or story, about why he should validate his phobia.

This lack of control is in nearly everything we do. Take for example the parent who disciplines their child and the way they execute the punishment. With all the constant traveling I have been doing, I have overheard many an argument through the hollow doors and walls of some hotels.

You'll find many parents discipline their children out of their own anger. This is why many parents use the counting method. That's really a sign of their own weakness and inability to control their own emotions. The scenario goes like this: "If you don't clean up your room now, one, two, two and half…" Then the child finally moves into action. And technically, the child moves into action because the parent is actually programming the child to believe not to listen to the parents on the first request, but to wait until the parent almost counts to three.

A lack of control is in nearly everything we do.

Often the reason a parent can't just administer discipline upon the first request is that they are not angry enough. It seems many parents wait to become angry at the child. This, in turn, allows the parent, in their own mind, to justify yelling or raising their voice or losing their temper. Whereas, if they had used more control, if the child didn't listen to them on the first request, with a still heart they could still administer the discipline or the consequences for not obeying.

For many people, due to their lack of control, it seems extremely counterintuitive to administer discipline to a child or a coworker with a calm heart or a still heart. Doing so takes a tremendous amount of self-control and self-awareness.

I mean, think about it. It's not easy to administer some kind of discipline when you are calm. It's as if we tell ourselves, 'Wait. Let me get a bit angrier so I feel justified in laying out the consequences of your behavior.' When you become more aware of your level of importance, it will suppress the weak mind that tells you that you must feel anger to administer discipline.

These are just a few of the many examples of how not understanding awareness and not understanding how to take better control of our nervous system actually ends up controlling us. In our next chapter, I will begin to give you more 'wax on, wax off' examples and exercises so you can begin practicing how to make your thoughts disappear.

We tend to forget, if we are even aware, of how important a role our nervous systems play in our lives for either good or bad. When something negative happens to us, and if we get caught up in the negative emotions of the situation, we are likely to start reacting in a negative way. That's just the way we are wired.

Then, the nervous system gets a negative charge. Your negative emotions will then build more and more. It's no different than the person who is phobic of a snake and every time they think of a snake they dig or ingrain the phobia deeper and deeper, negatively training their nervous system. Then they allow that fear to continue to fire off more negative emotions, feelings and unhelpful and inappropriate reactions.

When something negative happens to us, we are likely to start reacting in a negative way.

A person must be aware the moment this begins to happen. I'm often asked, "How do we stop this from happening?" My simple response is, "How did you start it? Now, do the opposite of your answer." I'll continue to use the snake example.

The more phobic or afraid of something a person is, the deeper and faster they keep ingraining the problem. Another scenario would involve the person who is phobic of a snake. At some point, they are totally calm and when you start talking about a snake, instantly that paints a picture in their mind and usually the first thing they do to reward that feeling is to change their breathing pattern, which often leads to an increased heart rate. The snowball will then begin rolling downhill, unless they first, force the change of their breathing patterns.

You have many opportunities, all day long, to learn to master this technique. Here is one of mine. With so much traveling in so many different cities, I have no idea what the speed limits are on each road I travel. I was recently pulled over by a local police officer. You know that feeling, right? I instantly stopped it from controlling me, and here is how I did that. I saw the lights from the police car and for most of us, that is immediately associated with a terrible, gut-wrenching feeling and an immediate change in breathing pattern.

The moment, the very moment, I saw the light, I instantly and quickly filled my lungs with air through my nose, thus immediately breaking the pattern of where I was about to go—the faster heart rate, the nervous anxiety and so on. Then, very slowly, I breathed out again through my nose, slowly letting it all out.

I have such a heightened awareness all of the time of my surroundings, my breathing, my thoughts and my emotions that, once I see that light from a police vehicle, I consciously adjust my breathing pattern in a matter of seconds. Now, for some people, this might seem trivial. But stop and think how many times in a day we could let external circumstances control us. This awareness gives us more control of how we choose to respond to things and offers us a better life.

It's this kind of awareness you will need to work on that will get you prepped to make your thoughts disappear.

Continuing with the example of being pulled over, some people talk about it after it happens for days. Then they make excuses for getting caught, and if they can't afford to pay the ticket they dig their emotional grave even deeper by complaining about the government and society in general. Some people even have to go get a drink because they are so upset. With my example of being totally aware and responding immediately, I accept the ticket and go about my merry way. Not only did I control the emotional side of my response, it also slowed or stopped the other negative snowball responses, making my day a better one in spite of the ticket. How many negative snowballs do you experience in a normal day that you don't catch in time to stop?

If we are not aware and don't stop the snowball effects with the example of a person having a phobic response to a snake, then next will be an increased heart rate, and perhaps screaming or running around like a crazy person. At that point all, your negative emotions have kicked in and they have just ingrained the phobia deeper into your nervous system. In the worst case scenario, the phobic person is now 100% totally out of control. Something else, of which that person is not even aware, the phobia has now taken total control of their emotions. Most people respond with similar patterns in other areas of their life on a day-to-day basis. It doesn't have to be related to a phobia.

It could be the thought of someone you dislike, which ingrains the dislike and disrupts your emotions more. It could be the memory of the loss of a loved one, or some other thought from your past. What negative thoughts or experiences do you have that the moment you start thinking about them, you end up racing down a negative road? When you ingrain the negative emotion, you make it worse, unless you stop along the trail and learn to release the negative emotion or at least change the meaning of it.

This is not to say you cannot or should not think about the loss of a loved one from your past. But you can still learn to have the thought and respond in a more positive manner, an emotionally and healthier way.

When you ingrain the negative emotion you make it worse.

I remember once flying on a commercial plane. We were about to take off, when I turned and looked over at a lady. As I looked over at her, I could tell she was afraid. She tightly grabbed the armrest. She actually lost awareness the moment she did that. We both knew that grabbing the armrest wouldn't change anything thing for the better. Subconsciously, due to her lack of awareness, she had just told herself, "I'm freaked out, let me prove it to you. Watch me grab the armrests as if I'm about to rip them off the seats and carry them off the plane."

That immediate reaction kicked in her nervous system and continued to make matters worse. The snowball effect continued and in her mind, her flying experience had been ruined while the four year old behind her was dying to get out from under the seat belt so he could get more of the amazing view from the windows that were too small to look through.

45

When I go up in my plane with people who have either a little or a large fear of flying, I will notice they often hold onto a strap attached to the inside cabin, that is designed to help pull them out of the seat to stand. Once they grab the strap, I will say to them, "Holding that strap doesn't make the fear go away." I tap their hand in an effort to help them let it go. The moment they do, they start taking control, whether they realize it or not.

One of the things I do at some of my seminars is to take a person from the audience who is extremely phobic, bring them on stage and use a process I have developed to reverse their phobia in minutes. How? My secret weapon. I retrain their central nervous system to use some of the methods I've already shared with you in this chapter.

YOU DON'T HAVE TO CONFRONT YOUR FEARS— THAT'S A MYTH!

I often hear people say something like, "If you want to get over your fears, you have to confront them." This is not necessarily true. When a person is truly phobic of something, just the mention of whatever their phobia is will create a negative response throughout their body. So, as they continue to think about whatever it is they are afraid of, the negative responses in them magnify. Then, the nervous system kicks in which in turn increases their heart rate, causes their palms to sweat and then, by the time they get even close to the real thing, their phobia is stronger and they are totally freaked out.

With the proper training, this person could learn to reprogram their reactions and thought processes just by understanding their nervous system better. Before they get to the focal point of their phobia, they would no longer have a negative reaction, as they did previously. Technically, it would no longer be considered a fear, let alone a phobia. This is extremely powerful. Essentially, the fear was removed before they confronted what it was they were originally afraid of.

You can learn to reprogram your reactions and thought processes just by understanding your nervous system better.

Many times during my events, when there are people who struggle with some phobia, they'll watch from the audience as I rewire or transform somebody onstage away from their phobia. Then, after the presentation, they will usually search me out and express how, before they came to the program, they were phobic of something specific but now, after watching this demonstration, their phobia is gone. This means they can now go up to whatever it was they were phobic of, and technically they're really not confronting the fear, because the fear has already been removed. That's extremely powerful.

I share all this with you because, to begin mastering and making your thoughts disappear, it requires total awareness—of your thoughts your feelings and your surroundings. If you're not aware of your day to day emotions and some of the things you can to do change them, you will never be able to make your thoughts disappear or come even close to controlling them.

I need to continue to emphasize the importance of not giving up because we're getting close to the specifics exercise. Again, I believe this concept is so new to some that many people can't even consider appreciating the benefits of mastering it.

47

As you begin making this a way of life, it becomes easier and easier. I've been at this for years. You will not master it right away. In time, you can become so conditioned to doing this on your own that you will program yourself, for example, at night to just fall asleep without consciously going through the exercises. It quickly becomes a habit—a good habit.

Just last night, I was lying down and meditating before going to sleep. Realizing I needed to get up early to continue to write this chapter for you, I started the first few steps of making my thoughts disappear. I don't even remember finishing the process. I was out like a light and I slept like a snoring baby.

It has become a natural part of my nightly behavioral pattern. For me, most of the time I wake up feeling so rested that my daily slate is wiped clean, ready to paint on a new canvas each day. I start each day without being pestered by the problems of yesterday. I like that feeling. It's another reason I made sure I learned to master this technique.

By following the exercises in this book, you'll take your awareness to a totally new level. I hope just this chapter alone helps you understand more about your nervous system, and helps you become more aware of how you let your negative thoughts and bad circumstances get worse by digging your emotional grave deeper. Stop that from happening—continue reading.

Chapter 5
WAX ON, WAX OFF TIME;
TIME TO TRAIN THE NERVOUS
SYSTEM

In the previous chapter, I introduced you to some concepts about the nervous system and how it can't tell the difference between imagination and reality. I'll be going into that subject more in-depth in this chapter.

Keep in mind the entire purpose of learning and understanding more about this subject is to dramatically increase your awareness. These are lessons of awareness I am consciously aware of throughout my entire day. You can become that aware of yourself, too.

Here are a few more exercises I do. I'm very observant of any controllable stress in my life. All stress is not bad for us. In fact, the right stress enables us to grow and thrive. One study at a college placed amoebas in a non-stressful environment where they had everything they needed. Amoeba life was perfect. A short while later, they all died while the control group of amoebae were placed under some stress. They all survived.

I recall reading a story. A company caught and shipped live fish across the country, but by the time the fish arrived at their destinations, all of the fish had died. Someone decided to solve that problem by subjecting the fish to some stress.

49

They added to the tank a species of fish that would continually chase the other fish around the tank. When they did that, all of the fish arrived alive, due to the added stress of being chased.

I work hard to manage negative stress and thrive on the positive things in life. Here is an example of negative stress. As I mentioned to you previously, I've been traveling consistently, every day, living in hotels for about three years. I can assure you you'd better learn to manage your stress if that lifestyle seems attractive to you, or you won't last long.

I have developed a huge love-hate relationship with my GPS. I can't tell you how often it has taken me in the wrong direction. If I have to give a presentation in a new city at a prescribed time and my GPS won't work right, and I see it could cause me to run late, you can imagine the stress level that will begin to cause.

Keep in mind, I am by no means immune to the same stresses and the same emotions that other people experience. I still want to master the necessary steps in preventing excessive stress from overwhelming me. I also want to learn to reverse the negative effects of stress.

So, in a situation like getting lost while driving my car, if the music is on, I instantly reach over and shut it off. Turning it off helps me control the stress of being lost and even later than I already may be. I will often feel my body heat increase so, immediately after that, I shut off the radio and decrease the temperature of the air conditioner to make it cooler inside the vehicle.

These are things I do consistently throughout my day to maintain control instead of allowing situations to control me. I'm constantly in defense mode when it comes to situations like this. I'd rather live this way then allow life to control me.

Another thing I do every time I have to drive, as a means of being consciously aware of my surroundings, emotions, feelings and the like, is control my facial muscles, especially on a sunny day.

On sunny days, we have a tendency to squint if we're not wearing sunglasses. I'm often aware of that in myself and I squint a lot more than I need to. So I'll instantly relax all of my facial muscles. I think you might be surprised how often your stress shows up in the muscles of your face and the expressions you make along with it. Squinting continues to induce more stress in the body.

Keep in mind, being conscious of this tendency to squint on a regular basis, and doing something about it, will keep you conditioned to be 'still of heart.' This adds to your quality of life, gives you more control and calms the spirit.

Here is something else you might come across. It seems a bit odd, but I'm hoping by now my ideas, if you're looking at the big picture, will continue to make more sense as you keep reading.

We have all been wired to be slaves to our feelings. When we feel sad, we act sad; when we feel happy, we act happy. What I am about to share with you is a lot easier said than done. When we feel sad, we should try to act happy. Why is this necessary and why is it so challenging?

This is perhaps one of the most powerful clues I can give you to help you master your behavior. Any time, and I repeat any time, you try to do something opposite of how you feel, and you will feel as if you are lying to yourself. As young children, most of us were trained or raised to believe lying is wrong.

We have all been wired
to be slaves to our feelings.

So, when you get to a crossroad in your mind, or with your emotions, whether it is a fear of failure, a fear of success, anger, or jealousy, you will have a tendency to take the path of least resistance. What is the path of least resistance when we experience negative feelings or emotions?

If you don't know this answer right off the tip of your tongue, I assure you, your emotions will control you instead of you controlling them. Unfortunately, that path of least resistance is a laundry list of negative emotions and giving in to any of them is the very worst thing any of us could do.

So then, why do we keep rewarding negative feelings and emotions? If we could just avoid giving in to our negative emotions just once, it would break the habit we have established by becoming angry or sullen or caustic. Once that habit or pattern is broken, it is so much easier to change the negative behavior and learn new habits, set new patterns that are positive in nature and rewarding by those around us who no longer have to run for cover when the situation becomes tense.

When we were born, one of the first things we started to do was to cry. So when we became hungry, we cried. When we had to use the bathroom we cried. After we eliminated our waste into our diapers, we cried again. There was just no pleasing us at that age! And how often did we do this in our first year of life? Hour after hour, day after day, week after week, month after month, as we became total slaves to our feelings.

But here's where it gets a little scary. We have been told the most impressionable part of our lives is usually the first five years. Do you realize, if this is true, we spend nearly half of the most impressionable part of our lives being total slaves to our feelings?

So now, if you ever wonder why it's so hard to lead your feelings as opposed to being a slave to them, now you have one of the answers.

ARE YOU A LEADER OF YOUR FEELINGS OR A SLAVE TO THEM?

So much of what I'm sharing with you in this book enables you to be a leader of your feelings and not a slave to them. Your life will be much happier and you will enjoy more control when you lead your feelings rather than being a slave of them.

I'm sure you've heard of people, when they get into bad situations, they ask somebody what they should do. Often somebody will say 'Follow your heart.' To me, it totally depends on the situation. Often, people end up following their hearts without leading their hearts, which gets them into a lot of trouble and a lot of pain—physical or emotional.

A typical example of this truth is in the area of relationships. I will often see people who have recently started a relationship and truly do love each other, but they both already know the relationship is not right for them and in fact is very unhealthy.

So, because they love the other person, they follow their heart instead of ignoring the signs that it's really not going to work out or it will end up being a very unhealthy relationship. In a case like this, the best thing might be that they lead their hearts and pull out of the relationship. Often, we feel, because we love somebody, we must follow our heart and try to solve the problem and fix the relationship, when in fact, it may be totally toxic.

The example or solution I offer people in a situation like this is to put the puppy to sleep. You may have a puppy or family animal that's dying of cancer or is experiencing a lot of pain. Though you love your pet dearly, unfortunately, you might have to put it to sleep. So in this particular case, you would be leading your feelings and not being a slave of them. The benefits of learning to lead your feelings are endless.

Because we are so naturally wired to be slaves to our feelings from birth, we often look for ways not to lead them, such as medication, alcohol and other things that might be unhealthy. Remember, I told you earlier about the preschoolers who are getting mood enhancing medications to help them deal with depression, hyperactivity and other psychiatric problems? This study came from the Journal of Psychiatric Services. This is crazy; something is totally wrong here! I mention it again, because I find it mind-numbing that so many people decide to medicate their children rather than looking for a more natural way of correcting problems.

Statistics have shown that depression will be the second largest killer in our society, behind heart disease, in the coming years. This is a dangerous epidemic in the world today. While I'm still on the subject, I've briefly given you my viewpoint on antidepressants and similar meds. I do believe from time to time it's necessary to have prescription medication, especially to stabilize someone.

But I think you will agree that it often becomes a crutch just like a bandage for a quick fix—QFS. It doesn't solve the core issues. Medication typically doesn't get to the root of the problem. It often just becomes the easy course of least resistance for both the doctor and the patient.

When life gets overwhelming, the ability to lead and master your emotions can make all the difference in the world.

I got off of my medication and muscle relaxers in my early 20s and haven't touched them since I started treating the core issues. I decided to become my own doctor and patient, if you will. And through understanding a few simple processes of behavior and how we think, I've been able to take back the control of my life by developing programs that do just that and helping others to do the same.

So when life gets overwhelming, the ability to lead and master your emotions can make all the difference in the world.

It's because of this very reason that I'm always looking for things in my day-to-day activities where I can find ways to condition myself to see and know that I am in control of my emotions. I had mentioned to you just a bit ago that we all have a tendency to be slaves to our feelings.

And one of the reasons it's hard to do the opposite of how we feel, such as feeling rejected and to move forward and not reward the rejection, is because we are wired to be slaves to our feelings. This again is also why it's so hard to feel sad and to try to act happy, though we know this is something we should do, which would give us more control and fight to keep the negative from getting worse.

DON'T WORRY, BE HAPPY...MOST OF THE TIME.

So here is something I do that I referred to you just a little bit earlier, that's a little unusual but once I share it with you I think you'll understand the principle behind it. So if I am in a situation where I get very excited and happy, I will instantly decrease or lower the excitement level both in my mind and throughout my body.

For example, if my face is showing excitement and I'm happy about something, in an instant I will change my facial expression to where I no longer show that excitement. Keep in mind, I do this in just an instant where you would never recognize it. If you had a video camera on me and replayed the video later, you might catch it very quickly. So I start off with the high level of excitement and the facial expression to show it drop it back down and then I take it back up, quickly.

Again why am I doing this? One of the reasons we have such a hard time controlling our behavior is because we are slaves to our feelings. So when we feel sad, we act sad, even though we know we should try to act happy when we feel sad. When we try to act happy, we feel as if we're lying to ourselves so we become slaves to that feeling and act sad, without continuing forward to try to change that.

So to counteract being a slave to our feelings, on the negative side of things, when we do feel sad, we should try to act happy. This is how we begin to rewire the way we think or feel. After I do this, on the other end of the spectrum I am consciously aware of being a leader of my feelings and not a slave of them.

When I feel extremely happy or excited, I will do the opposite of how I feel—lower the excitement and then bring it back up. Yes, this might, for most people, feel uncomfortable by feeling as if I'm lying to myself, because any time you try to do anything opposite to the way you feel, whether it is negative or positive, we will still feel as if we are lying to ourselves.

I hope you can now see the bigger picture of how these techniques and strategies keep you consciously aware of not only leading your feelings instead of being a slave to them, but also how they help you gain more control of your emotions.

Since we're such creatures of habit, I believe it's important to look for ways to be creative in breaking our patterns to enable us to change our behaviors or habits if they don't serve us well. Being a slave to your feelings, in my mind, is something that does not serve us well, especially if the feelings are not in harmony with our happiness and our goals.

There is still no way you can control your thoughts, much less make then disappear, without total awareness of your present state (thoughts and emotions). This will give you the option of controlling them or not, depending upon the situation. This understanding of the nervous system mentally primes you to consistently be conscious of what is going on with your thoughts, feelings and behaviors. This way, you can be more still of heart throughout your entire day, through starting the 'Wax on, Wax off' process.

Chapter 6
LET'S FIND YOUR SWEET SPOT

As an avid aviation fan and a certified flight instructor, I have to take courses of instruction every few years to maintain my licenses. I just recently renewed my flight instructor license and in that review course, one of the things I reviewed was what we refer to as 'drag.'

For example, if you've ever been on a commercial airliner in very cold weather, you'll note many times before they depart they have to spray down or de-ice the airplane. The reason they have to do that is because, if even a little bit of ice or snow gets built up on the wings or on any other exterior surface of the airplane, it creates a tremendous amount of drag.

This drag or snow can build up very quickly and often the aircraft will not have enough power to properly maintain safe flight speeds because the drag interrupts the flow of air over the wings to fly safely to our destination. Unfortunately, many accidents have happened because of this drag factor.

Let me illustrate how dangerous this can be. Just one grain of sand over a wing every square centimeter can cause up to 33% less performance on an airplane. Stop and think about that. Just a small grain of sand can cause that much drag on a powerful aircraft.

This means, if you were taking off and climbing through the air with one grain of sand on every one square centimeter, you would need as much as 33% more power to maintain your climb. The problem is you're already using full power to climb so you don't have any more power left. Unfortunately, this can cause an aircraft to stall and crash.

My hope for you in reading this book is that you will become much more aware of your own drag factor—your emotional drag factor. It works the same way. I often think of that small grain of sand causes so much drag on an aircraft when I think of our emotional drag.

I believe we all get this metaphoric sand in our own minds and that the grain of sand in our minds causing more emotional drag than the real drag causes on the airplane.

You will become much more aware of your own drag factor—your emotional drag factor.

With complete awareness, we can begin to immediately identify our emotional drag and either remove it or stop it from getting worse. I meet and talk with so many people that have so much emotional drag it ruins their lives or prevents them from achieving the happiness, health, relationships, and financial success they want and deserve.

When your life is in disarray, and you do not know how to get control of it again, you will often find yourself on an emotional roller coaster. When you are on that emotional roller coaster, you create emotional drag. When you have emotional drag, the smallest steps we need to take toward reaching your goals will feel as if you're pulling a one-thousand-pound ball.

Just like the airplane that needs so much energy to continue climbing through the air with that drag and many times it doesn't have enough extra power to do so, the same thing happens to us.

Emotional drag wears us down to the point we have no more power to continue going forward at the same pace we enjoy, or experience the happiness in life we need and deserve. I assure you, this book—my techniques—can help you reduce your emotional drag.

One way, perhaps, to illustrate this is to compare it to running a marathon with a 40-pound weight on each ankle. Once you remove the ankle weights, that drag factor, you will feel as if you're floating through the air. I often mentally experience 'floating through the air' so much throughout my day because I've learned to master my emotional drag to the point of removing it very quickly when it's on the surface of my mind.

Let's begin with our first exercise in helping you master your emotional drag. It's not rocket science, neither is it anything new. You've heard the expression before, 'Stop and smell the roses.' This really is a valuable lesson. We have so much going on in our day-to-day lives that we don't often take time to stop and smell the roses. One of the things you can do to immediately shed some of your emotional drag is to stop, or slow down and be still.

I recommend, at the very least, carving out two five-minute spots from your day to just stop, sit down, and relax. Anyone who makes the excuse they can't make time for this, definitely has a problem. And that problem will not go away by ignoring it.

This would be like the pilot saying he does not have time to de-ice the aircraft. The future of anyone who thinks like this can be easily predicted to be heading for an emotional stall and crash. Now keep in mind, I've never studied meditation. I am by no means an expert at this and I come to you totally from a layman's point of view.

The concept of taking these two 5-minute spots out of your day is to force yourself to identify any emotional drag you may be experiencing. I find too often that many people wait until it's too late to force themselves to do something like this. I believe you will mentally, physically, emotionally, and spiritually be much healthier by doing this before you think you need it.

Successful people create routines and habits that nurture their success. I encourage, you if you are not already doing this, to make it part of your daily routine or habit. By doing this, it primes or preps you like the 'Wax on, Wax off' principle. It is part of the first movement toward helping you prepare your thoughts to disappear at night before you go to sleep.

Successful people create routines and habits that nurture their success.

Even if you have no desire to continue pushing forward in this lesson on making your thoughts disappear, at the very least, please try these daily exercises for just one month. You will notice a positive change in your outlook and your ability to manage stress throughout the day.

I have found, in the most stressful times of my life, these exercises were incredibly beneficial and I give them a lot of credit for helping me slow down my mind and avoiding making my situation worse than it already was. These exercises made me slow down and remove some of the emotional drag I had accumulated in my life.

JUST SIT AND BE STILL

I will briefly go over this with you and then we'll elaborate on it later, as we go along. First, carve out a three to five minute period—from any part of your day—and go somewhere it is quiet. Even if you have to go into the bathroom stall or go outside somewhere and hide, that's fine, but just do it.

Let's say I have found a nice quiet room and I'm going to sit on a chair in this room. The first thing I do is close my eyes and position my body in such a way that I start to relax. I will discuss later some of the things I do to take my body from a very ecstatic and excited state to one of feeling totally relaxed. I go from one extreme to another in a matter of seconds. I control my body and mind to the point that I take it from one extreme to another in the snap of a finger.

I believe one of the most powerful means of taking control of your emotions starts with your breathing. In just a little bit, we're going to go over different ways to breathe and I think you might be quite surprised at just how powerful this can be. I use different breathing techniques, according to the amount of emotional drag I am experiencing, in my day-to-day activity. Often, the more intense the emotional drag, the more intense the breathing technique must be to deal with it.

So, now that we're sitting down, the first thing we want to do is to get our body into a very relaxed state. Understand, what works for me may not work for you, exactly. But the key here is to do something or put your body in some position so you instantly begin feeling relaxed, or at least feel some kind of relief, both mentally and physically. This will help you become present in the present moment. :)

Put your body in a position so you instantly begin feeling relaxed.

In addition to my breathing, the first thing I do is put my arms out, forearms on my thighs or on the arms of the chair, with my palms facing upward to the ceiling or the sky. I flex my hands several times to make sure I relax my fingers. I'll get back to the breathing in just a moment.

Pay very close attention to what I'm going to tell you next. One of your goals will be to go from walking around in your normal daily stressful lives, with the flood of thoughts that come with a normal day, and then just sit down. The change is almost like going from a sporting event to a stimulus deprivation chamber. Within seconds, you will go into a relaxed state of mind. Don't forget, that is your goal, but it may take some practice before experiencing your first success.

If you continue to work on mastering this simple technique throughout the day, it will become so much easier, when you are at the point of making your thoughts disappear, to help you control your thoughts before going to sleep. If you haven't yet created a pattern for doing this during the day, you're going to have a hard time mastering making your thoughts disappear when you need to go to sleep.

Earlier, I shared how, while driving, I am often aware of my facial muscles becoming tense, and how I can instantly relax those muscles. So while you're sitting down, I want you to start thinking

63

and asking yourself this question: 'Am I relaxed from head to toe?' Your goal should be to take an inventory of your body, from top to bottom, and start learning how to master the ability to relax every part of your body, very quickly.

Start with your facial muscles, then your head, your upper chest, torso, shoulders, arms, and finally your legs and feet. Once you've done this, it will be exciting; once you master this technique, you will develop the ability to make your thoughts disappear during your five-minute breaks. It's by far one of the best ways I know to quickly clear my mind during a hectic day.

Not only are you going to learn how to totally relax your mind and your body, you'll also take it to a whole new level of awareness by making your thoughts disappear, which will help you control your emotional stress, and make you feel rejuvenated, as if you've had an hour-long power nap. Power naps are usually most effective when they last only 15-20 minutes, so an entire hour of napping might make you feel extremely well and rested.

How can making your thoughts disappear for only a few minutes make you feel as if you've had an hour-long power nap? Haven't you been in a situation before when you were so emotionally stressed that you actually felt physically exhausted? That emotional pressure may have only lasted a few minutes, but I think we have all experienced some version of it.

When I am on stage, transforming someone to get rid of a phobia, when that person is changed, they feel mentally drained because of the emotional stress of clearing out the negative thoughts from their nervous system.

On the other hand, by concentrating for a short period of time on making your thoughts disappear, the reverse can also happen.

I believe another amazing by-product of learning how to make your thoughts disappear is that you can control when you need to sleep—although I personally no longer need a lot of sleep. The quality of my sleep is amazing. It is very deep so I am not interrupted through my sessions of four to six hours of sleep each night. When the quality of sleep is high, the quantity of sleep is not an issue.

What I will ask you to do in the next chapter is to practice some of these exercises. I'll also teach you more of these techniques. Then I would like you to take some time and sit down in a quiet area, find a comfortable position in which you can sit where your body feels relaxed.

Try what I do by having your palms face upward while resting your forearms on your thighs. I strongly encourage you to experiment with different positions until you find one that one best position that really puts you in a state of pure relaxation. That's what I call my 'sweet spot.'

Experiment and find a position that puts you in a state of pure relaxation. That's what I call my 'sweet spot.'

Don't rush this exercise; rather, take time finding your sweet spot. Once you have found it, your goal, whenever you need to relax, will be to return to that position, immediately. To get to my sweet spot when I'm sitting down, I instantly drop my shoulders and make my body whole go very limp. If I have no stress in my body, my shoulders will drop immediately, once I shrug them. You might want to try that —or something like it—as well.

65

When I shrug my shoulders, I will also relax my face, throat and chest, so the motion usually produces a sound something like a short moan or a 'harrumph.' That sound also serves as a sign that my relaxation is proceeding according to plan.

While sitting in the chair, I will sit with my hands open, my palms facing the ceiling and my thumbs facing away from each other. As

I take in a deep breath, I will slowly raise my hands off my thighs (just a little) and turn my wrists so my palms are facing my thighs and my thumbs are facing each other. Then I will slowly exhale and simultaneously lower my hands, turning my wrists again, so my palms are facing up again when I lower them against my thighs again with the completion of the exhale. I will do that for three to five minutes, deepening my state of relaxation all the while.

Sometimes, people have trouble—for whatever the reason—and need some additional opportunities. If you think this describes your initial experiences, consider joining me in my Self-Esteem Program at unbreakableselfesteem.com.

For the best opportunities to learn and grow with a personal trainer, go to garycoxe.com/go/beyond-first-class materials.

Let's not stop here. You're on a roll, so let's get to the next chapter and begin these exercises while they are still fresh in your mind.

Chapter 7
THE BREATH OF LIFE
IMPROVES WITH PRACTICE

Hopefully, you have already found your sweet spot. The next thing we're going to do is to go through some more breathing techniques. Keep in mind, in the exercise in which you look for your best position to relax in, keep doing an inventory of your muscles—tight or relaxed- -from head to toes, to get your entire body to relax. Your ultimate goal is to get to that point of total relaxation in just a few seconds, but that may take some practice, so don't get discouraged during your first few attempts.

As we continue to build on this subject, we're also going to discuss certain times in your day that you will have to find different kinds of sweet spots or positions you can get yourself into, to create another focus for relaxation.

For example, we'll search for one position you can use in your car and another lying down just before bedtime as you begin working on making your thoughts disappear.

You may recall in a previous chapter, I told you how a nurse asked me, while she was taking my pulse, if I was actually controlling my heart rate and slowing it down. That's exactly what I was doing. The ability to have that level of control comes from consciously going from an excited state from a discouraged state to one of sitting down and instantly relaxing literally in just a matter of a few seconds. I want you to make this one of your goals—to be able to relax your entire body in just a few minutes and ultimately in just a few seconds.

As a reminder, find regular times to get into your sweet spot, like while looking for a quiet place twice a day. Then use the breathing techniques and the relaxation techniques I'm sharing with you. This is all part of the 'Wax on, Wax off' process that is setting you up to do a better job of mastering your ability to make your thoughts disappear, whenever you want to do so.

BENEFITS AND POWER BEHIND THE RIGHT BREATHING METHODS

There is so much more to breathing than meets the eye. The correct kind of breathing not only can relax you, but it is one of the most powerful pattern-breakers available. Here's what I mean by that. The moment you have a negative thought, or whenever something negative happens to you when you find yourself in a negative experience, one of the first things to change without even realizing it, is your breathing pattern.

As I mentioned earlier, one of the keys to incredible control is awareness. You want to get to the point of responding so quickly— in a few seconds or less—that you instantly break the negative breathing patterns that induce or reward your negative behaviors. The more immediate your reaction, the greater the rewards you will enjoy by doing it.

There are many reasons why this is so powerful and important. Keep in mind, if we don't stop interrupting our negative behaviors, such as negative breathing patterns, then the nervous system takes over and digs your grave deeper and deeper, making your situation go from bad to worse by taking over your reactions and making you say or do things you may end up regretting later.

The 'Wax on, Wax off' process sets you up to master making your thoughts disappear whenever you need.

What I'm going to do is share a different breathing method with you. This is the one I use and I want to encourage you to try it as well. I'm also going to have you create your own technique, one that might work best for you, personally. We will start off with the time we're going to put aside—at least twice a day for a few minutes each time to just relax and meditate.

Once I have found the sweet spot where I feel at ease, in this particular case sitting with my palms facing toward the ceiling or upward, then I start my basic breathing exercise. First, I close my eyes to eliminate any visual stimulation. If you're not looking at the picture sitting lopsided on the wall, or those socks on the floor (which you should have already picked up), you will have a better chance of really relaxing. Then I take a deep breath—just through my nose—and fill up my lungs. The next thing may seem a little bit unusual, but for me it really keeps me mentally connected. Sometimes, I will first start with my palms facing down and then turn them slowly as I raise my hands a few inches above my lap as I inhale.

As I'm raising my hands, slowly breathing in through my nose, I will stop raising my hands when I have filled my lungs with air. When my lungs are full, I briefly hold my breath for one or two seconds, keeping my palms facing the ceiling. Then I will slowly bring my palms back down onto my legs or onto the arms of the chair, depending on what kind of situation I am in, and at the same time slowly breathe out again, through my nose only.

Depending on the situation when I sit down, I may just go ahead and sit with my palms facing up, again placing my forearms on my lap. Most of the time, I choose to first fill my lungs with air by breathing through my nose and simultaneously, I will turn my palms upward and raise my hands about three inches above my thighs, hold my breath for about one or two seconds before releasing the air from my lungs and slowing bringing my hands back down to rest, as my palms still face upward.

Before we practice again, let me explain more about the purpose of moving the hands. You may begin with your hands in either a palms up or palms down position on your lap. It doesn't really matter. The rhythmic movement of your hands going from palms up to palms down is helpful in teaching you to focus on your body. Once you become confident in your ability to relax, you no longer have to move your hands—unless you still find it helpful.

Again, for emphasis, the steps start with taking air in through my nose, to fill up my lungs. I will start with my palms facing down, so my thumbs are facing toward each other. Then I will simultaneously raise my hands about 3 inches above my thighs, until I've completely filled my lungs. Then, I will hold my breath for about one or two seconds and slowly release the air through my nose as I bring my hands back down to rest in a palms-upward position on my lap.

Relaxation Sequence—Variation 1 (Sitting)

1. Sit comfortably in a chair with your hands on your thighs—palms down.
2. Close your eyes and breathe in through your nose only, filling your lungs with air.
3. While inhaling through nose, raise your hands 2 to 3

inches above your thighs and turn your palms downward. When your lungs are full, stop raising your hands. Raise and lower your hands only once, to establish your rhythm.

4. When your lungs are full, hold your breath for 1-2 seconds with hands remaining above your lap.
5. Slowly exhale all the air from your lungs while turning your palms upward and lowering your hands back to your thighs.
6. Repeat this sequence for 1-2 minutes or as long as it takes for you to feel relaxed.

STEP ONE
RELAX ALL YOUR MUSCLES

STEP 2
INHALE AND FILL LUNGS. RAISE HANDS FROM LAP
HOLD BREATH FOR 1 SECOND

STEP 3
TURN HANDS SO PALMS ARE UP.
EXHALE

STEP 4
CONTINUE EXHALING.
TURN PALMS UP

STEP 5
COMPLETE EXHALE AND REST HANDS
PALMS DOWN ON YOUR LAP

SLEEP IN A NORMAL POSITION

Since we normally do not breathe this way, any time you do it, you create an immediate change in your normal breathing pattern which will instantly help you relax, or at least slow you down. This is something you can do 10 to 20 times a day, if you like. You can do it if you're sitting down, lying down or even standing. Of course, you will get better results by sitting down because your body is more relaxed, but you can do it anytime and in almost any position.

Now that you have done this exercise, whether you realize it or not, you have broken any type of breathing pattern you previously had before doing the exercise. Whether it's from a normal breathing pattern you have had throughout the day, or an intense breathing pattern brought about by some negative stimulus that was a pattern you learned in your past.

The next thing to do is to continue slowly breathing in and out through your nose. Then just simply relax the muscle of your body. As you're doing this, start becoming consciously aware of all your muscles—especially any tense muscles from your head to your toes. When you find them, start relaxing them.

I will usually close my eyes and drop my shoulders into a very relaxed state. For me, personally, as I'm sitting down, I actually go directly to being totally relaxed and I can barely hold my body up in the chair because I have been practicing this technique for years. I frequently do this after my first exhale of air, once my hands have come back down to my lap.

When you find muscles that are still tight, immediately start relaxing them.

Keep in mind, as we continue throughout this book, we're going to get to the point of doing it from a very relaxed state and then getting to where you can work on making your thoughts disappear.

If you find you have a problem sitting and relaxing in a chair, then try it lying down. You can lie on a bed. The exact location does not matter as much as the attempt to find your sweet spot.

When I lie down, I lie on my back on the bed. I will typically put my arms out to my sides with the elbows bent at about 90 degrees and touching the bed. My hands will be closer to my head than to my feet.

When you first try this position, do not try of force your hands to touch the bed. As you relax on the bed, you will find your hands and wrists will relax closer to the bed, about six inches above the bed and one to two feet away from your ears. The goal is to allow your hands and wrists to hang limp in the air beside your head. In fact, I use that stiffness in my hands and wrists to measure my state of relaxation. I know when my hands are hanging limp, I am relaxed and ready to continue.

Relaxation Sequence—Variation 3

1. Lie down on your back, in your comfortable bed with your elbows bent about 90 degrees and your hands near the bed, closer to your shoulders—palms up.

2. Close your eyes and breathe only through your nose as you inhale and fill your lungs with air.

3. When your lungs are full of air, hold your breath for 1-2 seconds.

4. Slowly exhale, simultaneously allowing your arms to relax until they are closer to the bed, beside your head—palms up.

5. Repeat sequence for 1-2 minutes, or as long as it takes for you to feel relaxed.

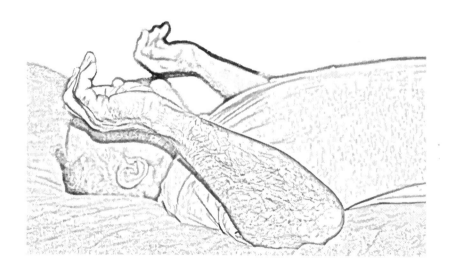

STEPS 1-3
LIE ON YOUR BACK WITH ARMS BENT
HANDS NEAR YOUR SHOULDERS, PALMS UP
CLOSE YOUR EYES
BREATHE DEEPLY
WHEN LUNGS ARE FULL, HOLD BREATH FOR 2 SECS

STEPS 4-5
EXHALE DEEPLY, RELAX YOUR MUSCLES
YOUR HANDS AND WRISTS WILL GO LIMP

I have been doing this routine for years, so I no longer have to go through all the steps. But it may be a while before you get to that point. While you are learning this exercise, you may need to follow the routine below to help you relax every part of your body.

Relaxation Script:

- Concentrate on relaxing your breathing, your face and your forehead.

- Concentrate on relaxing your upper back, your chest and your neck.

- Concentrate on relaxing your buttocks, your groin, and your abdominals.

- Concentrate on relaxing your thighs, your knees and your calves, and your thighs

- Concentrate on relaxing your ankles, your feet and your toes.

- Now concentrate on relaxing your entire body, more and more with each breath; deeper and deeper, relaxing even more with each breath you take.

- Relax all you muscles, top to bottom with each breath; relax left to right with every breath; relax front to back with each breath you take. Until you are totally relaxed, feeling every muscle of your body from the crown of your head to the soles of your feet as they go limp and you are relaxed.

Because this technique is probably new to you, consider recording the steps from the script and listening to them as you are lying down. You might also have someone read the script in a soft and soothing voice so you can hear it. The results will be the same. You may find it more useful to record your voice in a nice slow pace, reading those instructions so you don't have to interrupt yourself to read them. Maybe a partner will read them to you and give you feedback afterward about what they might have observed as you either relaxed or resisted during the exercise, so you can improve each time you do it.

At this point, even if you never master the ability to make your thoughts disappear, this particular exercise is something you should repeat daily, until you learn to master it as a solid part of your daily routine. But for right now, just focus on getting your body accustomed to relaxing without worrying about getting to the next level of making your thoughts disappear.

What I would like you to do this time is to put this book down and go ahead and practice this exercise so you can get the feeling of what it's like to put your body and mind into a state of total relaxation. Remember too, your goal is to get into this relaxed position as quickly as you possibly can, once you begin the process.

But, before you put your book down to practice, let's rehearse it one more time. So one more time, let's go over it again.

Eyes closed, sitting comfortably, palms facing down in your lap. Fill your lungs with as much air as possible through your nose only and, simultaneously, start slowly raising your hands from your lap and turn your palms to face upward. Initially, your thumbs will be pointing toward each other. Then move them to pointing straight upward, so your thumbs will be pointing toward each other and lying in your lap, once the repetition is completed.

As you are doing this, you're slowly raising your palms just a few inches, to stop when your lungs are full of air. When they're full, stop raising your palms. Hold your breath for just about a second or two, and then slowly exhale the air from your lungs as you simultaneously bring your palms back down until they are again facing upward against a resting area, whether on your lap, the couch or the chair you're sitting on, or wherever else you may be sitting.

After you've gotten to this point, all you want to do is continue to breathe in slowly through your nose, hold your breath for just about a second, making sure your lungs are totally filled, and then slowly release the air again. As you're doing this, you're also trying to identify any areas of your body that might still be tense so you can do something to help you relax them, or allow them to become very limp.

With regards to allowing your body to be limp, it's important to be sitting on a chair with back support so you can go limp and rest against it as you become much more relaxed.

I'm sure you have often seen people with their legs crossed, sitting on a beach or somewhere else, meditating, without a couch or chair, and they are keeping their back totally straight. This is obviously not like that. When your back is totally straight, you cannot be very relaxed and I find, for me, that takes me to a whole different level of relaxation.

Now it's your turn to try this exercise. Go ahead and do it now.

So, how did you do? If you did it correctly, you should feel an immediate difference in your body's level of tenseness and a decreased feeling of anxiety.

PLAY WITH YOUR BREATHING

I use different breathing techniques for different situations. The more intense the situation, the more intense the breathing technique I will use to interrupt the negative breathing pattern from whatever intense situation I might have just experienced.

I would define an intense situation as something that instantly and quickly changes your breathing patterns and also dramatically increases your heart rate and feelings of anxiety. This could be anything from a car accident, to somebody yelling at you, to being pulled over by a police officer, or anything that causes your patterns of breathing and heart rate to change—situations you might associate as negative or causing you to feel as if you are losing control.

The more intense the situation, the more intense the breathing technique to interrupt negative breathing patterns.

In our previous exercise, we had our eyes closed and then we slowly filled up our lungs with air by breathing only through the nose. Common sense tells us there will be times when you obviously cannot close your eyes—especially if you're driving, flying or doing something else that requires you to watch for your own safety.

So imagine you suddenly get involved in a very intense situation and the moment it starts, you automatically change your breathing or anxiety level. You go into a different and more intense breathing pattern. For example, using common sense, if I'm able, I will close my eyes Then I will fill up my lungs with air through my nose, but this time I will do it faster. And then I might hold my breath a little bit longer—maybe for 3 to 5 seconds.

The next thing I do is designed to go a bit overboard to break that intense negative breathing pattern I have just experienced, or maybe slow down my breathing to counter some negative situation. I will slowly exhale that air through my nose, but then I will purge all the air from my lungs.

In other words, I will slowly let some air out of my lungs for about half of a second, then pause and hold my breath. I will purge it again for another half second or less, then pause, hold my breath and continue to do that until only about three quarters of my air has been exhaled.

Then the last quarter of air that's left in my lungs, I will slowly let out until it's completely released, without stopping, as I did just previously. As I'm doing this, I can actually feel my lungs deflate. I will continue to inhale and quickly deflate my lungs every time and repeat this until the exercise is complete and I am ready and able to deal with whatever situation I am faced with. The more intense the situation, the more I will repeat the pattern. This may take as little as 30 seconds or as much as 2-3 minutes.

Recall earlier in the book I told you about my friend, Dean, who would have himself buried in the sand with water poured on the sand so he could feel the restricted movement of his chest every time he inhaled and exhaled. These exercises were designed to give him total awareness of what is going on in his body and throughout his lungs and chest. The quicker you are aware of your response to something negative, the faster you will be able to interrupt the stressful, downward spiral by using breathing techniques like this.

Perhaps you've done something similar to what Dean was taught either when you were a child or even as an adult. Picture yourself laying in your bathtub and when you fill up your lungs completely, your body will rise to the top of the water because you're becoming more buoyant. Slowly let out all the air and you'll see your body slowly sink down into the water again because you've become less buoyant. In the extreme breathing exercise I just shared with you, as I purge the air from my lungs, I will feel my lungs slowly start to empty as I continue to let out the air.

Keep in mind, I do this now by habit, without really thinking much about it when I'm confronted with an intense emotional situation.

Don't forget the wisdom and the purpose behind doing something like these exercises. It will immediately stop or break the pattern of your mind, body and emotions from going down the continual negative path brought on by the negative situation. Not to mention, this technique either stops, slows down, or removes the emotional drag you would have built up because of the negative situation that could be escalating around you.

I do this now by habit, whenever I'm confronted with an intense emotional situation.

Let's do a quick review of this exercise and then I'll have you stop and try it for yourself. Fill your lungs with air through your nose only and do it faster than in the relaxed exercise I described previously. Hold your breath at bit longer, about 3 to 5 seconds, and at the same time, move your hands in rhythm with your breathing.

Remember, if you are planning to continue using the palms up or down technique, you will start with your palms facing down, both thumbs facing toward each other. Then, as you inhale faster, filling your lungs, you will turn your palms upward faster than in the previous exercise and then stop as you raise your palms when your lungs are full.

Then, slowly release the air from your lungs through your nose only. As you're purging the air, only releasing it for about a half a second, simultaneously drop your palms and at the same time, stop moving your hands when you start holding your breath again. Slowly release the air again for about a half a second and pause as you're simultaneously lowering your palms for the next repetition, and so on. I will usually do this about three times or until three quarters of the air in my lungs is purged. The last quarter of air in my lungs, I will slowly exhale through my nose, approximately three times slower than in the previous purging.

As I'm doing this breathing exercise, I am also making sure I remain totally aware of all other parts of my body that may be stressed or tensed, such as the muscles of my legs, my back, my shoulders, my face and so on.

In just a moment, I'll have you try this exercise. Keep in mind this is an exercise I use for intense situations. This is my SWAT team exercise, so to speak. In an intense situation, it gets the job done— and prepares me quickly for a tough situation. You can practice this particular exercise at any time and use it whenever you want without any problems. You may do that for practice if you like. But keep it in your quiver as your weapon of last resort and don't be afraid to use it.

But, it works best if you use it only when you need to call upon it after you have learned how to do it quickly, without having to think about it. Again, it's part of the 'Wax on, Wax off' process. It takes practice and you must allow it to become a way of life before expecting your body and mind to work together to help you in emergencies.

Now it's your time to practice the exercise. Let's see how you do. Go ahead and begin now.

How did you do? I hope you were able to figure it out and that you will remember the power of this incredible technique. It provides several advantages for you. First, it helps you to take more control whenever you want. Second, it helps to break negative patterns that would otherwise take you down the emotional road that you don't want to travel. And by the way, this is a technique I use often when I'm driving, if somebody cuts in front of me and I come close to having an accident or anything similar that brings me closer to an emotional problem I know would be very negative.

I'm going to strongly encourage you to practice these exercises 5 to 10 times for the first few days, just to get into the routine and to make the process more familiar to you. After that, performing them just two to time each day and once just before bedtime, for just a few minutes each time, will be sufficient to help you. The reason I want you to do this more regularly than normal is because I want you to create a routine or a pattern and make this a way of life with which you can instantly know how to use these exercises when you need them—and even when you don't—to maintain an emotional balance.

Perform these exercises 2 to 3 times each day, for just a few minutes each time.

Well, we are getting a lot closer to the next step of making your thoughts disappear. But first, let's talk a little bit more about the benefits of exercises like these how they affect your emotional balance.

Chapter 8
AN INTERVIEW WITH YOURSELF

Not only are these exercises a great way to stop and break the fast paced patterns we all too often force ourselves to live, but I also look at them as a meditation technique. I frequently think of meditation as an interview with myself. So, in addition to using these exercise techniques to relax, I also want you to use them as a way of interviewing yourself throughout the day.

All interviews are done with questions. So, now it's time to ask yourself a list of questions. This is a great way to start your day, so you can design your day just the way you like it—and also so you can be more prepared when the day you planned becomes nothing like the day that emerges. After all, we can't predict everything and often our greatest plans fall apart when the unexpected falls into our laps.

Ask yourself questions similar to the ones below:

Am I at peace with others and myself? This question needs an answer. Judaism includes in their culture annual holiday to get rid of bad feelings and old anger between you and anyone else you might have offended. The day is Yom Kippur. It is the day every year when they will individually face the people they may have offended during the past year and apologize for any offense, imagined or real. What a cleansing opportunity to start over again—and to do it better next time. I wish more people could muster the courage it takes to face a person you offended, confess the offense and ask for forgiveness. Imagine starting a new year without the inner rage and bitterness that comes when people keep offenses inside—perceived or real—for years and years and years.

Are my relationships with the people closest to me healthy, positive and productive? You can usually choose the people you have around you—even family. If you don't get along with your spouse or your children you are the one who is the best position to change that. Children look to their parents for examples of how to behave in society. If your children don't show love (it is an action verb) or respect for you, consider the example they see when you think they aren't watching. Become the kind of parent they want you to be and watch your family come together. It won't happen overnight, and it may even take years before your example sinks in, but it will happen.

Am I happy with the person I am becoming? You can blame your parents—or the lack of parents—all you want, but it does not change the fact that you can become the person you want to be. If you take a look around you, you will see people in all socio-economic groups who are happy—or at least content with what they have. Sure, you will also find people of all strata who are angry, bitter and upset at the world for the life they are forced to live. But blaming society or anyone else will never help lift that person out of their bitterness. If you are not the person you want to be, take an inventory of your perceived short-comings and study them until you understand why you feel that way then find a way to change the negative ones so you can become a more positive, successful and likable person.

Do I enjoy keeping my own company? If you don't even like yourself, how can you expect other people to like you? I have met a lot of people who want to blame society for their troubles, when the truth is they are just not the kind of person anyone else wants to spend time with. When the lights go out and everyone else has gone to their homes, all you have left is yourself. If you don't like yourself today, then admit to yourself why that is so and start working on ways to fix that problem. You have every right to like keeping your own company and you should enjoy your time with yourself as well as your time with family and friends. If you don't, then get off your duff and fix it.

Am I happy with the amount of time I am putting into my job, career or business each day and the quality of work I am performing? It is common for people in our society to dislike the job they go to every day, five or six days each week. I will frequently hear the excuse that "It puts bread on the table." Or "I have a family to support, so it doesn't matter whether I like my job or not." My favorite excuse is, "I'm too old to start looking for another job. No one wants to hire an older person." In other words, these people are trapped—or at least they feel trapped. I think they are just lacking passion. Passion for their job, passion for their lifestyle and maybe even passion for life itself. This is the 21st century. Anyone who believes they have no choices in the kind of job they work is just not being honest with themselves. But it takes passion—passion and a sense of adventure because it is a big risk to throw away everything you have built over the years. But whatever the size of the empire you have built yourself, it will not do you any good if you are dead at the age of 35 or 50 because the stress of your job gives you a heart attack. These techniques can help you find peace of mind in whatever circumstances you find yourself until you can arrange your life the way you want it, to enjoy every day more than ever before.

Am I doing everything I can for my health? Don't rationalize your health problems and think they can't be improved. Don't tell yourself (again) that dieting is too difficult, you've tried to quit smoking and it's just too hard, or you have no time to exercise. Don't settle for anything less than healthy. Again, this is the 21st century. Medicine and nutritional understand and appreciation have never been better than they are today and you can do whatever you need to take control of your life. But you have to start somewhere. Where do you want to start? What kinds of change do you want to achieve first? How about starting from where you are today?

Never forget, you cannot change what you do not acknowledge. I will often use these exercises to reflect upon and to determine what is weighing heavy on my heart and my mind. I think it's also very important to understand when a person does not make time to do things like this, they're not creating a life for themselves by design, due to the fact they're not willing to see what is wrong so they can fix it.

You cannot change what you do not acknowledge.

People like me, who create a life by design, take time to stop and reflect on the world and their place in it. They use this time to reflect on many things. To figuratively pull in the reins, they reflect on where they find they may be going off course, a bit. Reflection can also help you identify why you're choosing to maintain such a fast pace in life, without choosing to take just a few minutes of your day to stop and smell the roses. For many people, the reason they don't stop and take time to do things like this is that they're hiding something mentally or emotionally—or both.

By not taking the time to reflect, they will end up suppressing negative emotions that ultimately will surface and will need to be dealt with. What are you masking or hiding from your heart? In the world and in the society that we live in today, we are busy becoming antisocial by constantly hiding behind text messaging, emails, social media and other technological advances.

I think one of the greatest advantages of doing these relaxation exercises and meditation a few times a day, is that it forces you to have more balance in your day-to-day activities and in your life as a whole. If you find something as simple as grabbing a few minutes a day for yourself, then I am going to guess you might have too much on your plate and you have not placed enough value on any of it to remove some of it and apply the discipline needed to create more balance in your life.

If this is something you do not do regularly, or that you might find challenging, ask yourself a few questions: What causes me to think I'm so busy I can't make time to have more balance in my life? What are my excuses and my stories I keep telling myself, or the things I might be hiding from that, if I took time to slow down and reflect, I might open up Pandora's Box?

The content in this book is not designed to help you deal with the kinds of things you might find in your version of Pandora's Box. That would be a subject for another book. If reflecting on your day or your life brings up an emotional pain, that is a sure sign you need some healing or something is clogging up your emotional hard drive.

If this healing isn't done, eventually, you will become more callous to your problems and then emotional gangrene will set in. Use these exercises—and exercises like them—as a way to listen to your heart, mind and body. Another question you could ask yourself is, 'What am I afraid of?' Some people may experience tears as they reflect on their life, due to whatever is happening in their present life or whatever happened in their past. Use those tears to wash your heart, mind and spirit. They were given to us for a reason.

Simplify your life so you can find time to breathe. Never forget, success equals time. If you take a moment right now to identify anybody who is successful in any area of their life, one thing they all have in common is that they have spent a lot of time becoming successful in that special area of their life.

It would be reasonable to assume we would all like to be successful in all areas of our life—or at least in one area—such as our finances, our relationships, our health, our spirituality and more. But the biggest danger I see, is when people become really unbalanced. Many times, people are very successful in at least one area of their life and very unsuccessful in most other areas because they have too much on their plate and not enough balance. So they do not dedicate enough time to each one of these areas to be successful in them.

If you don't even have enough time to carve out for two five-minute sessions for yourself, you have too much on your plate. I would be willing to bet your life may not be totally successful in all the areas that we just mentioned above. One of the missing

links may be you don't have enough balance in your life because you have too much on your plate. Or there might be some things that you could remove to find more balance and be even more successful and happier. To do this takes time and effort.

This is where you have to stop, reflect and ask yourself what your real values are and your priorities in life. If you find your priorities are out of balance, believe me, you are missing out. I hope this book, to some degree, helps you become more aware of your real values and priorities and, more importantly, motivates you to do something about it.

I often look for additional ways in my daily routine that I can stop and pump the brakes on my life. In my travels, I will often be driving and when I see a beautiful flower or a lovely animal. I will just pull over and stop to enjoy it, video it, or just take a single picture. This is my way of slowing down my daily routine, because it's often extremely busy and fast-paced. Doing little things like this regularly and consistently creates awareness for me to slow down and change my patterns of behavior as needed.

BE PREPARED TO ABORT OR TAKEOFF

I also use these exercises to try to look ahead into my day, if I do them in the morning, to see what challenges or problems might arise. I do this to make sure I'm ready for just about anything and to make sure I am mentally and emotionally prepared to manage or counteract the challenges of the day.

I'll explain to you in a moment how I do this. Perhaps you're going through a divorce. You might have lost a loved one. A holiday or a birthday coming up after a loved one died and will no longer be with you. Maybe you have a lawsuit, a court date or something else negative happening in your life.

Here's how to manage problems like this. One of the things I do as a pilot, before takeoff, while on the runway, is to add the throttle and say out loud to myself and to my copilot, "Be prepared to abort or to lose an engine!" I often have those who fly with me wear headsets so they can listen in on the conversations going on inside the cockpit. Those who might have a slight fear of flying sometimes get a mental jolt when they hear that statement.

For some people, hearing such a statement like "Be prepared to abort or to lose an engine," may appear to be quite negative—oh, all right, it may scare the heebie-jeebies out them. But ultimately, it's very realistic. You could think about it this way. When you put on the seatbelt inside your car, is that negative or realistic? Of course, it's realistic. I hope you realize, we're not actually saying to ourselves as we put on the seatbelt "I'm doing this because I might have an accident." The real reason we do it is because it's the law. So essentially, we are saying, "Be prepared to abort or to have an accident." Nothing negative about it. It's just smart.

"Be prepared to abort or to lose an engine!"

Right before takeoff, when I say this, I don't say it as if I'm scared to death or that it's really going to happen. I say it to create the mindset that I'm ready, just in case something negative does happen. Who would you rather fly with, a pilot who has simulated many engine emergencies, or a pilot who has never simulated a single one?

Do you recall in an earlier chapter what I referred to as my secret weapon? Yes, it was the human nervous system. Remember, the nervous system cannot tell the difference between imagination and reality. So, let's take that knowledge and use it in our relaxation or meditation exercises. Here is how I do this, and it is very powerful.

As I'm sitting down relaxing, if I reflect on something negative, I will mentally walk through and role-play the possibilities in my mind. Remember, the nervous system cannot tell the difference between imagination and reality. As I walk through a predictably negative part of my day, such as you might have going to court or having some other situation that's going to create a lot of negative emotions, keep in mind, the emotions you think about will start triggering endorphins in your nervous system.

Maybe you have to fire someone and find that a difficult situation. That could breed anxiety inside of you, along with increased heart rate, blood pressure and other like natural physiological responses.

This is exactly what you want to happen. You would rather have this happen while you're sitting down relaxing, so you can start mentally controlling the negative emotions that might be coming up. How would you do that?

As you think about what it is that's going to bring up these negative emotions, you will note, if you are aware, that just the thought of it alone will start changing your breathing pattern in a negative way. You might also experience a negative breathing pattern if you were to be pulled over to the side of the road by a police officer. As you're thinking about what the police officer might do to you, you start breaking your learned breathing pattern and interrupting it with new pattern, though you're not actually experiencing it right now. You're only thinking about it, and remember, just thinking about it will create a reaction because the nervous system cannot tell the difference between imagination and reality.

This is extremely powerful. Keep in mind, many people won't stop and do exercises like this because they are afraid of self-reflection and of feeling these negative emotions until they have no choice. But whether they realize it or not, these emotions are going to hit them, sooner later. If they are not prepared to meet them, those emotions will take control of them instead of allowing them to remain in control of their own emotions.

This is actually something like what Tiger Woods' father did with him, to help him become an incredible golfer. While Tiger was a young child, his father created exercises that helped him increase his focus on his strokes.

Many people won't do exercises like this because they are afraid of feeling negative emotions.

For example, one of the things his father did was, while Tiger was getting ready to putt, he got close to him and made a lot of noise, yelled at him as if he were pretending to be part of a crowd and purposely distracting him so he would learn to ignore the noise and stay focused.

Whereas, somebody else might want to say, 'Oh, be very quiet. Don't make any noise. Tiger is getting ready to putt.' This is a totally different contrast to how most golf classes are taught, with totally different results.

I recently saw another example of this principle. It was on one of those TV shows where people get to audition their singing skills. A well-known artist was working with somebody who had a problem with nervousness singing in front of people or in front of a large crowd.

So this famous artist told the person she was coaching, to practice with the radio or the TV blaring loudly, to learn how to perform with distractions. But the concept was to practice with a pretend audience before you get in front of a real audience. She was actually helping her train to control the nervous system because it can't tell the difference between imagination and reality.

In this particular example, the artist was creating a scenario where it was still somewhat real, like the distraction of the loud music or the TV. The person being coached could then take it to another level by imagining the distraction. How do we know that works? Because the nervous system cannot tell the difference between imagination and reality.

So, just as I prepare for the possibility of something negative to happen at take-off, I also use this exercise to mentally prepare me for my day, in case something happens that I'm not expecting. There is a point in our lives that the stress becomes so great we don't even want to go through a single day because we have so many negative things waiting to ambush us.

But we get up anyway, and unfortunately, we end up fighting those problems. If we would only take the time and do an exercise like this every morning, especially knowing we're going to have an incredibly stressful day, we would be able to counteract the negative emotions before it's too late. I would just think about the problems, and as they bring up negative feelings, I would go from a negative breathing pattern to stopping and controlling my breathing pattern, through the exercises I shared with you in the previous chapter.

When you do this, the real problem happens later in the day. The advantage you have is that you have already started to rewire yourself to prepare for the possibility of those negative emotions. And now, if done correctly, you won't make your emotional snowball roll downhill and make the situation grow and grow. You will be prepared in advance to stop the insanity before it starts. I cannot express to you enough how powerful this is when you take it to an incredible level of self-mastery.

You have already started to rewire yourself to prepare for the possibility of those negative emotions.

I speak from experience. As a reminder, my experience comes from everything from infidelity of a spouse and subsequent divorce, to having my uncle killed in a plane crash. From my grandfather and stepfather dying of cancer, to my father being murdered. And all of that happened by the time I was 21 years old.

Then there was the losing of my so-called friends and family after I chose to leave a tightly knit religious sect, being entirely on my own and having to totally reconstruct my entire value and belief system.

This all nearly took me to the point of bankruptcy—emotional and financial. I could go on and on with the list of tragedies that have happened to me, but one thing I can assure you is, I have tapped into my ability to control my nervous system, understanding that it cannot tell the difference between imagination and reality. I believe it is the ultimate tool to show us how to play games with your mind rather than allowing your mind to play games with you.

As I reflect on all these challenges, as crazy as this may sound, the most painful experience of my life was dealing with losing all my so-called friends and family, and reconstructing my entire value and belief system. Sadly, it made the tragedies in my life seem like a cakewalk.

I just want you to know I understand your challenges. I have devoted my life to sharing my ideas and strategies with people, to help them learn to deal with their challenges so they can be happier and more fulfilled. One of the more important things is to help them remove the pain from their lives. I've experienced so much pain in my life that I have been blessed, and that enables me to walk in the shoes of many people—including you.

Though I would rather have not experienced all the tragedies I have had in my life, the blessings coupled with finding the right attitude, as I went through those tragedies and now look back at them, they are priceless and immeasurable. I believe God has given me the greatest gift of all and that's the gift to help other people move forward from their past, learn to put their past behind them, to become more successful in life. Together, let's not run away from our open wounds but let's learn to heal them and become the kind of person we really want to become.

Chapter 9
HOW TO DAY DREAM AT NIGHT

I want you to think back to a point when you remember what it was like to daydream. Essentially, daydreaming is a short-term detachment from your immediate surroundings. You seem to be consciously aware of your surroundings, but essentially, your mind is blank, or detached from reality for a few moments.

Even though when you daydream you don't consciously plan to do it, it just happens, and for the moment you've made your thoughts disappear. Though you are awake and conscious, you're really not thinking about anything.

When people daydream, they don't do it in a very excited state. The state of mind or body of a daydreamer is one that is usually still and relatively relaxed or calm. Perhaps the best way to explain what it's like to make your thoughts disappear is by comparing it to daydreaming.

The key now is to learn how to put yourself in a state of daydreaming. Some people actually refer to it as a trance, for lack of a better word, and they use that state of mind to consciously make your thoughts disappear for a longer period of time.

If you could, for example, cause yourself to daydream when you want to, you could detach from 'reality' at will. Please don't take this literally, as if I'm encouraging you not to deal with your problems at hand. That's not it at all. Understand, if we can control the time and place we "daydream," what we actually could be doing is stopping or interrupting a negative pattern of emotions or feelings occurring at that very moment.

99

So far, we've gone over exercises that have been preparing you to meditate and slowing down by taking breaks throughout the day and by doing the exercises we discussed in previous chapters. This, in and of itself, will be a great benefit to you.

Now, let's take this to the next level—the level of making your thoughts disappear while you're sitting down in a relaxed state. So, now we're going to discuss how to make yourself daydream at will, whenever you want to.

What we will actually do now is to build on the previous exercises. Then, after we learn how to relax our mind and body, we will then learn how to make our thoughts disappear. In other words, we're going to start today, daydreaming whenever we want to. That's really a nice thought, isn't it? Because daydreams are usually very pleasant. Then, we're going to take the next step and build on that.

We're going to start today, daydreaming whenever we want to.

That step involves taking the knowledge we've gained so far and applying it when we want to sleep, but can't. Once mastered, you will actually teach yourself to daydream at night, to the point of falling asleep quickly.

By far, this is the most difficult part of the exercise—yes, to actually make your thoughts disappear. Let me now go in greater detail about what I actually mean by making your thoughts disappear in the following scenarios.

You will be able to sit down, stop and relax and then totally eliminate any specific thoughts from your mind. You'll be consciously aware of what's going on around you, but you will not be actively thinking about them.

I'll be the first to tell you, this is not an easy thing to do because it is so uniquely foreign to the majority of the population.

It's now time to begin.

Before explaining the process of actually learning how to make your thoughts disappear, we must first get our bodies and our minds into a very relaxed state. This is what we've been doing up to this point. So, before we walk through the specific step-by-step process, let me explain one more time how this is done. Then we will go into detail to actually start practicing it.

YOU CAN'T CHASE TWO THOUGHTS AT ONCE
Confucius said, 'Man who chases two rabbits, catches none. This applies to our thought process as well. We can't consciously think of two thoughts simultaneously—just like you can't drive in two different directions at the same time with one vehicle.

Now, think for a moment why many people get extremely stressed or have a hard time sleeping. One of these reasons is that they're mind is being flooded with too many thoughts. The best way I know to illustrate this is comparing it to one of those money booths you might see on a game show on TV.

Confucius said, 'Man who chases two rabbits, catches none.'

Imagine you have been put into this money booth where you're locked up in a see-through Plexiglas box. Once you're in there, a fan that is beneath the floor of the booth you are in starts blowing the money all over the box. Your goal now is to try to grab as much money as you can while the money is being blown around by the fan.

The actual challenge of this activity is built around the fact that it's very difficult for you to catch the money because it's moving all over the place. Now, if you could ethically cheat—as if there were such a thing—the simplest way to walk out of that booth with as much money in your hands as possible would be to shut off the fan. Obviously, when you do that, all the money falls to the floor and then you can easily scoop it up.

Our thoughts work in a similar manner. Any time you find yourself mentally stressed, one of the reasons for this is because you often have too many thoughts flying around your mind and it's hard for you to control them. This can be induced by high emotions, or even lower emotions—meaning few if any feelings about what is happening around you or to you.

So, using the analogy of the money box, what could we do to help eliminate some of these stressed feelings of being overwhelmed? Simply put, shut off the fan. In other words, slow down, stop, take the time to put your thoughts together, either writing them on paper or just by slowing down your mind. Slow the movements of your thoughts. In the exercises we have been doing, we've discussed exactly how those exercises will enable you to do this.

It's no different than when I shared earlier, about my traveling with a lot of things going on around me. Then, when I get to a rental car, I might be running behind schedule, and this additional stress assaults me. The last thing I want to do is to add more stress to myself by taking phone calls or turning on the radio or any other distractions.

So, the moment I feel some stress in a scenario or situation like this, if the radio is on, I immediately shut it off. This enables me to slow things down and coordinate my thoughts better.

Now that we've discussed taking ourselves to the next level where we learn to relax the body and the mind through breathing techniques, and relaxing the muscles all over the body, it's time to work on controlling the specific thoughts and then ultimately making them disappear.

First, we'll assume you're in that relaxed state in your chair. Okay, your eyes are closed. I'm sharing with you the simple things that will follow. Then we'll get to the details on how to make this all happen.

The next step, of course, is to make your thoughts disappear. We now have to take all of our thoughts and stop them in their tracks. Without lots of training and practice, at this point it is still not practical to assume you could do it—yet.

So, let's start on funneling your thoughts to just one particular thought. Let's go a step further and just think about one word. That's right just one word. I would prefer you pick a word that describes something tangible to which you associate no meaning and no feelings. It needs to be completely neutral. A pen, a watch, a chair, a tree, or a glass.

Once you have picked your object, your goal will be to slowly repeat it over and over in your mind. This is how you'll get your mind to begin to stop thinking about anything else and narrow it down to only one item. Don't forget, it's extremely difficult to consciously and simultaneously think of two things at one time.

Many people in our society have bought into the modern day myth of multi-tasking. Some job announcements and job interviewers even ask whether the applicant is able to multi-task as a pre-requisite of being hired for that position. Psychologists have recently determined that this highly sought after ability to engage in several activities simultaneously or to manage several different events at the same time is, in fact, simply a myth. It is not possible.

Whenever we try to do several things at the same time, we are actually giving less attention to all of them and are unable to truly focus on any of them. The end result is that we finish several jobs with less efficiency than if we had been working on just one of them at a time. We finish reading several books with less understanding of any of them than if we had read just one of them at a time.

Let's return to the word you selected, on which you will focus all of your attention.

The speed at which you will say this word is important. You don't want to say it so quickly that it keeps you from your relaxed state. But, on the other hand, you don't want to say it so slowly that you have time for other thoughts to creep into your consciousness in between repetitions.

Psychologists have recently determined that multi-tasking, or engaging in several activities simultaneously is simply a myth.

I just gave you the final clue of what you are just starting to master. Your goal now is to simply say that word slowly in your mind,
over and over again, so it is the only thing you are focusing on. Leave no space between each repetition of that word. If you do, this is when you'll end up allowing other thoughts to creep into your mind. This is what you don't want to happen.

YOUR 3-MINUTE CHALLENGE

I want you to practice this at least twice a day every day, and one additional time right before you go to bed. Do this while lying down in your bed. Say the word for 3 minutes straight, without interruption.

What happens if I stop before the three minutes have finished? If you do stop, you must start all over again. This exercise is to get you conditioned to slowing down and staying focused on one thought and one thought only. If you can't even slow down for three minutes, and focus on one thought, you'll never be able to focus on no thoughts at all. Wax on, wax off. Remember?

You must also avoid allowing anything else to enter your mind. This is the real challenge. If you think of any other word or thought, consider it a failure and you didn't pass the test. Now, start all over again.

I have to do this for several days? How many days? The real answer is: until you can go for at least 3 minutes saying that one simple one word, with no other words or thoughts coming into your mind. If you find three minutes is too long to start off with, then begin with only one minute intervals and work your way up to three minutes.

Once you've mastered this relaxation technique, then you're ready for the next level—and you only have two more levels to go. Now it's time for you to increase the interval between the times you say the words you have been repeating to yourself. Up to this point, this has been your most difficult challenge.

Instead of saying the words slowly over and over again repeatedly, one after another, your goal will now change pausing for a few seconds between words without letting other thoughts come into your mind during that short space of time.

Before we start practicing your 3-minute challenge, I want to warn you, if you haven't yet mastered repeating your word over and over for any length of time, and kept yourself from being distracted by letting other thoughts inside, then this 3-minute challenge will be a total waste of time. This next step is very difficult.

Let's run a scenario sample test, first. Here is how this will go. I'm going to use the word 'pen.' Assuming I've passed step one, now I must consistently repeat that one word for a specific length of time, without allowing other thoughts to interrupt the slow repetition of that word.

Once you are totally relaxed with your eyes closed, you will say to yourself, 'pen.' Then pause for only a few seconds before saying it again. The goal is to avoid letting any stray thoughts come into your mind during those few seconds. No thought whatsoever. Only, do it for as long as you can, without a single stray thought becoming between repetitions of your word.

Consistently repeat one word for a specific length of time, without allowing other thoughts to interrupt your repetition.

You might only be able to do this for three-second intervals. If so, keep doing the 3-second intervals and keep doing it for about a minute. Once you've mastered the three-second mark, stretch it out to about 5 or 10 seconds. Master that level, and then stretch it again and again for longer intervals.

Your eventual goal will be to remove the 'pen' from your thoughts…totally. No thoughts at all. Not even any thoughts of the pen—no thoughts of thinking any thoughts at all! Don't even think about it! :)

Clearing Thoughts Technique Variation 1

1. Get into your Sweet Spot—sitting with your forearms resting on your lap. Your fingers should be extended with your palms either up or down on your lap.

2. Breathe deep—slowly inhale and exhale, simultaneously raising and lowering your hands and turning your wrists from palms up to palms down. Remember to stop breathing for one or two seconds when your lungs are full of air.

3. Continue repeating that sequence until you feel your body is totally relaxed.

4. Begin thinking of the word for your chosen
    item. Repeat that word over and over in your
    mind. Time your thinking of the word to
    your breathing—two to five times with each
    inhalation and two to five times with each
    exhalation.

5. Slow down the speed of repeating that word
    until you have stopped thinking about
    anything and everything all together.

Clearing Thoughts Technique
Variation 2

1. Get into your Sweet Spot—lying on your
    back with your elbows bent and your hands
    closer to your head than your feet.

2. Breathe deep—slowly inhale and exhale.
    With each exhalation, feel your arms relax
    until your hands are resting beside your head.
    Remember to stop breathing for one or two
    seconds when your lungs are full of air.

3.　Continue repeating that sequence until you feel your body is totally relaxed.

4.　Begin thinking of the word for your chosen item. Repeat that word over and over in your mind. Time your thinking of the word to your breathing—two to five times with each inhalation and two to five times with each exhalation.

5.　Slow down the speed of repeating that word until you have stopped thinking about anything and everything all together.

How did it go the first time? It will take some practice, but I can tell you are the kind of person who can achieve disappearing your thoughts because you finished this entire book, and did the exercises along the way. Congratulations!

If you achieved your goal, that still does not make you a master of your emotions. But it means you are on the right track. You are on your way to success because you now have the tools you need to overcome obstacles that you may encounter at any time in life.

None of us are immune to such obstacles. None of us can predict when they will come, what kind of obstacles they may be or whether we will fall prey to them at all. But now you have the tools—the weapons—to prepare yourself and to overcome them when they occur.

When I do these techniques at bedtime, after lying down I first clear mind, then I say my prayers. After that time of communion, I relax and go to sleep. Somewhere in the night, I roll over onto my side, but I truthfully don't remember doing it any more. If you are not a back sleeper and want to roll onto your side after relaxing in bed on your back, then try to do so with as little movement as possible so you don't wake yourself up.

The idea of doing this at bedtime is to help you get a glorious and good night's sleep without having to drink one or two hot toddies, take one or two pills, or read for hours before you fall asleep from exhaustion.

Good night.

Chapter 10
What You Have Achieved

In chapter one, you learned about the kinds of things in life that lead people to even greater problems if they lose their temper, become vengeful or give up hope. The inability to manage stress of any kind often leads people to alcohol or drug addiction for artificial relief. This can happen no matter how mild or severe the stress. Just the perception of overwhelming stress sometimes makes people fall apart.

I shared examples from my past about how bad life can get and I confessed how I did not initially handle my stresses well. But I finally decided I was not going to allow my emotions and my past control me. Rather, I found ways to control my stress and that was what brought me to this career field and to writing this book for you.

In chapter two, I explained how vitally important it is for all of us to be aware of what is going on in our minds and with our bodies and what is going on all around us. Without this awareness, we can easily become prey to our emotions when bad things happen— and emotional displays rarely make a situation better.

I compared your awareness to a muscle and explained how your awareness needs to be acknowledged and worked, stretched and stressed—like a muscle—in order to increase its strength and ability. I also reminded you of something people sometimes forget—or they stop believing when they are suddenly hurled into a stressful environment. The human body and mind are capable of so much more than we now understand. We just need to learn to listen and pay attention when they try to warn us of impending problems.

You already have the strength within you to overcome obstacles and perform feats of strength and skill, but you have not known where to look for those hidden reservoirs that are surely within you. I hope this chapter helped you to understand and be more aware of your potential for good.

In chapter three, we discussed ancient philosophies that indicate the human body and brain can live a lot longer than we can comprehend right now. Somewhere along the line, we lost that knowledge, but now we know the potential is definitely within us. When we have the knowledge of how to live intelligently and make the wise decisions necessary to take better care of ourselves, we will find that living past one hundred years of age will become a common occurrence instead of the exception.

The food we eat, the exercise we engage in, the way we treat the people around us and the way we manage stress all have a major impact on how healthy we are and how productive we can be throughout our lives and especially through our golden years.

In chapter four, you learned more about the human nervous system. The human brain and nervous system are the most highly developed and complicated organs in the known universe. Yet the nervous system cannot tell the difference between what is imagined and what is real. It will respond to any stimulus as if it were real and end up scaring a person into believing they are in danger when, in fact, they are not.

Learning how to harness the power of our brain and take control of our nervous system allows us to take control of our lives. If you have ever lost that control—even just momentarily—then you already know how frightening that can be. Maintaining control of our minds, bodies and emotions is a major step toward greater longevity and greater happiness and prosperity.

In chapter five, I started showing you ways to learn how to control your nervous system. I explained how we are all naturally pre-disposed to being slaves to our emotions. As infants, our emotions got us the attention we needed to be fed, changed and loved. As we grew older, we discovered it was no longer cute to make a fuss in public.

In learning how to lead our emotions and become their masters, we are taking greater control of our lives. There is nothing attractive about an adult who throws temper tantrums or makes a scene of any kind in order to get attention. When you have control of your life, you are more secure in the attention you already get and you know you are doing well in life.

In chapter six, you learned about the different kinds of emotional drag you may have been carrying around for years and years. I explained how difficult it becomes to carry around your old stories and explained the advantages of getting rid of your old, negative stories and creating new and positive ones—stories which will remind you of the principles you are learning in this book and principles which will help you maintain control of your life.

You started looking for your own Sweet spot—that position in which you can attain the greatest relaxation. I showed you some breathing exercises and helped you prepare yourself for greater learning, greater relaxation and greater control. I hope you discovered how wonderful relaxing can be and how little effort it really takes in order to relax.

In chapter seven, you received some specific guidance on ways to relax and sleep better. In this chapter, you learned some options available to you. You also learned that, when you can sit quietly for a few minutes at least twice each day, you can meditate, breathe and relax. At the end of each day, or whenever you get the chance to lie down, you can relax all of the muscles in your body and prepare yourself for a good night's sleep.

In chapter eight, you received a list of questions to use to interview yourself while you are meditating. Remember, meditation is not an excuse to escape from the world; it's a way to recharge your battery so you can face the world more effectively. Asking yourself those questions is a way to help you understand your current place in the world and to show you how to improve your lot in life.

If you do not acknowledge your shortcomings and faults, your weaknesses and strengths, you will need to do so before you can attain that control of your life that you want so much. Do not be afraid to face your negative attributes—especially your negative emotions. Facing them, acknowledging them and changing them into positive attributes is the way to gain control of your life.

In chapter nine, I finally showed you how to disappear your thoughts—how to make them vanish so you can think more clearly during the day and sleep more restfully at night. I hope you really tried those exercises because the positive results of learning to do them well are all-encompassing and wonderful.

If you find it difficult to multi-task, don't worry. You can still choose one task at a time and do it so much better than the multi-tasters who will forever believe they can do everything at the same time and end up doing none of them as well as if they had only one task.

I have truly enjoyed this opportunity to share some of the techniques I have learned over the years, to help you overcome the challenges life may throw at you.

These techniques can—and will—help you when you need them most. If you continue practicing them on a daily basis and improving your ability to use them on short notice, they will be available to you when you need them.

These techniques can—and will—help you when you need them most, if you continue practicing them on a daily basis and improving your ability to use them on short notice.

If you find you want to continue studying my techniques, go online to garycoxe.com and see the other reading material, seminars and opportunities available for you to become the best possible You.

Take care,
Your friend and Coach,
Gary

48684382R00066

Made in the USA
Lexington, KY
09 January 2016